ACPL ITEM
DISCARDED

641.57
Quantity,
S0-DSF-828

Quantity Food Production

Disclaimer

The information presented in this skillbook has been compiled from sources and documents believed to be reliable and represents the best professional judgment of The Educational Foundation of the National Restaurant Association. However, the accuracy of the information presented is not guaranteed, nor is any responsibility assumed or implied by The Educational Foundation for any damage or loss resulting from inaccuracies or omissions.

Allen County Public Library
900 Webster Street
PO Box 2270
Fort Wayne, IN 46801-2270

Quantity Food Production Skillbook

Copyright © 1993 by The Educational Foundation of the National Restaurant Association.

All rights reserved. No part of this publication may be reproduced, stored in a retrieval system, or transmitted in any form or by any means, electronic, mechanical, photocopying, recording, or otherwise, without the prior written permission of the publisher.

On behalf of the people in the foodservice industry who will benefit, The Educational Foundation is pleased to thank

The Pepsi-Cola Company

for the financial support which has made possible the development of this book.

Pepsi and Pepsi-Cola are registered trademarks of PepsiCo, Inc.

Contents

INTRODUCTION

About the Management Skills Program

The Management Skills Program is designed to help foodservice and hospitality managers and supervisors build and improve the specific skills they need to manage operations. The skillbooks included in the Program are divided into five functional areas of foodservice management:

Operations Management

Human Resources Management

Administrative Management

Financial Management

Marketing Management

To receive a Foodservice Management Skills Certificate, managers must pass five exams, one in each functional area. As participants successfully complete individual exams, they will be awarded certificates for those functional areas.

How to Use This Skillbook

Read the material in the skillbook carefully, completing the progress checks that appear throughout. Answers are in the back of the skillbook. Make notes as you read, and refer to the skillbook often as you refine your supervisory and management skills. When you have finished reading the skillbook, complete the Test Your Knowledge, which will help you prepare if you choose to take the exam for this functional area.

About The Educational Foundation

The Management Skills Program is offered by The Educational Foundation of the National Restaurant Association, which is dedicated to developing outstanding training programs for the foodservice industry. For more information on training programs, call The Foundation at 312/715–1010 or 800/765–2122.

Training Objectives

After completing this skillbook, you should be able to:

- Identify methods of managing and maintaining safe and sanitary kitchen conditions.
- Explain how nutritional considerations affect purchasing, food preparation, and menu planning.
- Match kitchen tools and equipment to tasks, and describe tool and equipment maintenance techniques.
- List appropriate methods of selecting, preparing, and cooking meat, poultry, and seafood.
- Explain how to prepare cold meats, garde-manger foods, stocks, soups, and sauces.
- Explain how to select and prepare fruits and vegetables to maintain their highest quality.
- Describe techniques for preparing potatoes, grains, and pasta.
- Explain how to select, store, and handle nonperishable foods to maintain their highest quality.
- Explain how to select and prepare dairy products and breakfast foods.
- Describe how to prepare hors d'oeuvres, appetizers, salads, and bakery products.
- Describe how to prepare various bakery products using demonstrated methods and techniques.

PREPARING THE PROFESSIONAL KITCHEN

Managing a Sanitary and Safe Kitchen

In food service, the importance of maintaining sanitary and safe conditions cannot be overemphasized. Unsanitary and careless work habits can cause foodborne illnesses that can be dangerous to customers and to a restaurant's reputation. In food service, *sanitation* refers to creating and maintaining conditions favorable to good health. Many of these conditions are regulated by federal, state, and local agencies.

Food can serve as a potential carrier for many different illnesses, with the severity depending on the amount of contaminated food consumed and the individual's immune system. The cause of food contamination can be chemical, physical, or biological. For example, chemical tainting can be caused by insecticides or cleaning compounds; physical contamination can be caused by rodent hairs or glass pieces; biological contaminants can be caused by naturally occurring toxins found in rhubarb leaves and green potatoes.

Biological sources account for the majority of foodborne illnesses. *Pathogens* (disease-causing micro-organisms) are responsible for up to 95 percent of all foodborne illnesses. Five conditions control the growth of micro-organisms:

- Protein source
- Readily available moisture
- Moderate pH
- Available oxygen
- Storage temperature

The higher the amount of protein in a food, the greater its potential as a carrier of foodborne illness. That is why meats, poultry, seafood, tofu, and dairy products (except for some hard cheeses) are considered potentially hazardous foods.

Many foodborne illnesses are the result of unsanitary handling conditions in the kitchen. *Cross-contamination* occurs when disease-causing elements are transferred from one contaminated surface to another. There are several ways to prevent outbreaks of foodborne illness:

- Personal cleanliness is one of the best defenses against cross-contamination. Kitchen employees must wash their hands any time they come in contact with a possible source of contamination.
- Careful preparation and storage of food can eliminate cross-contamination. Equipment and cutting boards must be properly cleaned and sanitized between uses.

- Proper cooling methods with strict time/temperature controls are essential. The food *temperature danger zone* is the temperature range in which foods are most susceptible to microbial contamination, from 45°F to 140°F (7°C to 60°C). Any food left in the danger zone for more than four hours is considered unfit to eat. (See Exhibit 1.)
- Reheated foods must move through the temperature danger zone as rapidly as possible and be brought to a safe internal temperature before serving.
- Frozen foods should be thawed under refrigeration and used as soon as possible.
- Foods stored in refrigerators and freezers should be kept at the proper temperature.

  Meat and poultry—32°F to 36°F (0°C to 2°C)

  Fish and shellfish—30°F to 34°F (−1°C to 1°C)

  Eggs—38°F to 40°F (3°C to 4°C)

  Dairy products—36°F to 40°F (2°C to 4°C)

  Produce—40°F to 45°F (4°C to 7°C)
- Foods kept in dry storage should be in a well-ventilated, clean area. Refrigerated, frozen, and dry stored foods should be used based on the *first in, first out (FIFO)* inventory method.
- All tableware and equipment must be properly cleaned and sanitized. *Cleaning* means the removal of oil and food particles. *Sanitizing* means using moist heat or chemical agents to kill pathogenic microorganisms.

Safety measures are necessary to prevent accidents to staff and guests. Here are some guidelines:

- Clean up grease and other spills as they occur.
- Beware of grill fires.
- Observe caution when changing the oil in deep-fat fryers.
- Keep fire extinguishers accessible and in working order.
- Train all staff in the Heimlich maneuver.
- Handle all equipment carefully.
- Never work under the influence of alcohol or drugs.
- Put emergency phone numbers near every phone.

EXHIBIT 1—TEMPERATURES AND THEIR RELATIONS TO FOOD

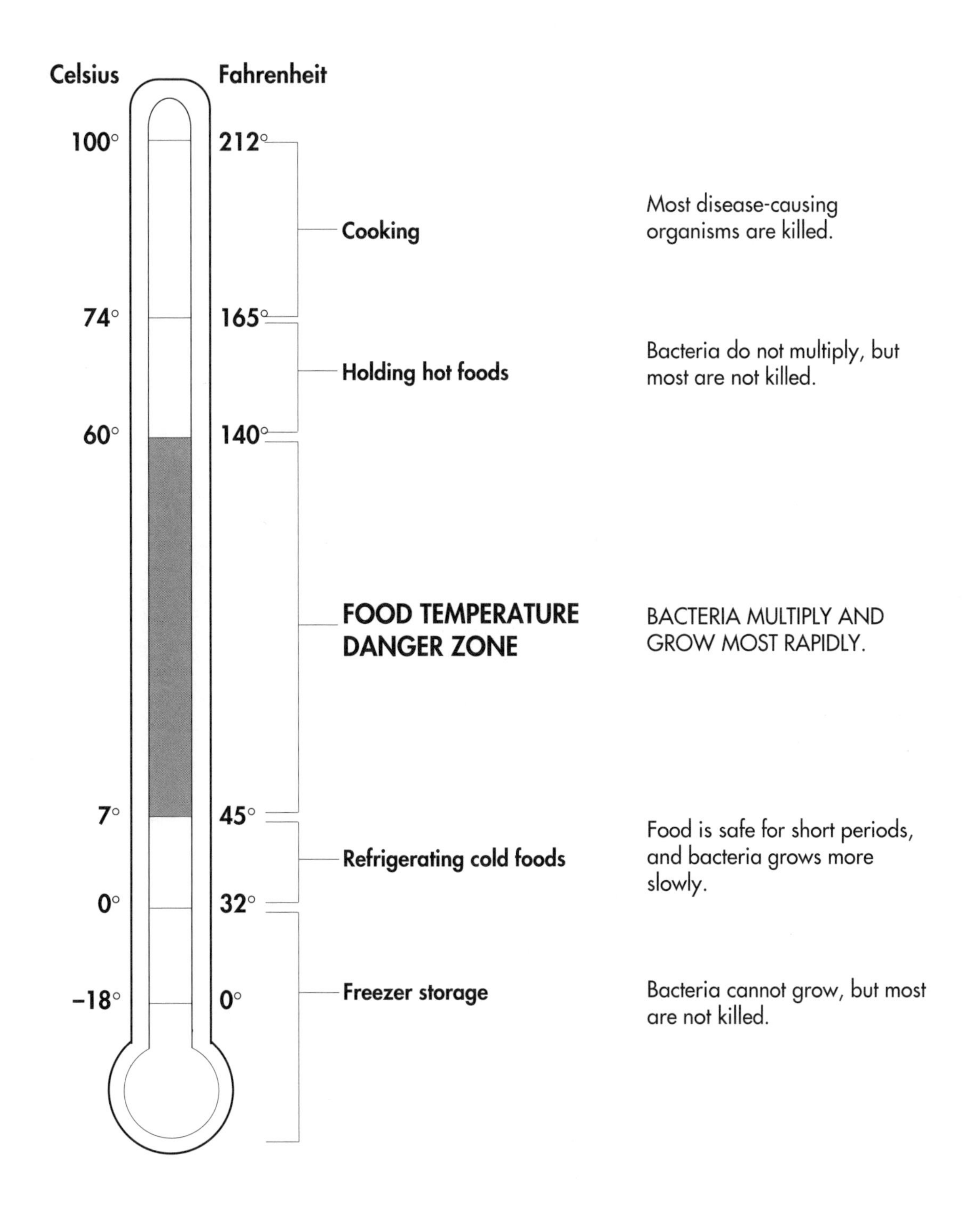

Nutrition in Quantity Cooking

Nutrition greatly affects the way foods are selected, prepared, and presented. Consumers' increasing consciousness of what they eat has made eating nutritious foods very popular. The successful chef must continually create new healthful ways of preparing food.

There are six basic nutrients:

1. Carbohydrates
2. Proteins
3. Fats
4. Vitamins
5. Minerals
6. Water

Carbohydrates are valuable energy sources found in foods such as potatoes and cereals. *Proteins* are composed of nitrogen-containing chemical compounds called amino acids. The human body needs 22 different amino acids to function properly. Fourteen are manufactured by the body; the remaining eight must be supplied through diet. The essential function of *fats* is to provide flavor, a feeling of fullness, and energy. There are three classifications of fats: *saturated* (increase cholesterol levels in the blood), *polyunsaturated*, and *monounsaturated* (either lower cholesterol levels or have no effect).

Vitamins are key in the regulation of many biological functions as well as in the release of energy from calories. *Minerals* are essential for healthy bones and muscles, heartbeat regularity, fluid balance, oxygen flow, and nerve impulses. The federal government's *Recommended Daily Allowance (RDA)* establishes suggested amounts of proteins, vitamins, and minerals.

Why are health and nutrition important to foodservice managers? Health-conscious patrons are increasingly well educated about foods and expect a restaurant's menu to reflect their dietary concerns. The first step is to plan a menu that includes healthy choices, such as:

- Fresh produce
- Low-fat dairy products
- Foods cooked in poly- or monounsaturated oils
- Dishes prepared with legumes and grains
- Fish entrées
- Substituting herbs and spices for salt when possible
- Eliminating food additives

Once these foods are purchased, it is essential to store them properly so that they retain their nutrients. Exposure to air, heat, and water should be kept at a minimum until immediately prior to cooking. Following are some suggestions for preparing food in a healthy way:

- Establish correct portion sizes.
- Cook vegetables for the shortest amount of time, in the least amount of liquid.
- Use cooking techniques that do not require using fats and oils, such as poaching, steaming, roasting, and grilling.
- Select sauces to enhance the overall flavor and color of the dish.
- Use nutritionally sound recipes and modify existing recipes to reflect healthy concerns. Often, fat can be reduced or completely eliminated. A few suggestions: substitute evaporated skim milk for heavy cream in soup and sauce recipes; use grains, vegetables, and legumes to stuff items, rather than traditional forcemeats that might include a high percentage of fat; use egg whites rather than whole eggs where possible.
- Highlight nutritional entrées on the menu.

Foodservice Equipment

The selection, use, and care of various kitchen tools and equipment are essential in mastering basic cooking techniques. The professional chef must be familiar with the various types of kitchen equipment and their uses.

The only piece of equipment more basic to cooking than the knife is the human hand. (See Exhibit 2.) The following rules are essential for proper use and care of knives:

- Keep knives sharp.
- Keep knives clean, and sanitize as necessary.
- Use an appropriate cutting surface.
- Use a knife for its intended purpose only.

EXHIBIT 2—TYPES OF KNIVES

TYPE OF KNIFE	USE
Chef's knife or French knife	All purpose
Utility knife	Light cutting chores
Paring knife	Paring and trimming vegetables and fruits
Boning knife	Separating raw meat from the bone
Filleting knife	Filleting fish

(continues page 8)

EXHIBIT 2—continued

TYPE OF KNIFE	USE
Slicer	Slicing cooked meat
Cleaver	Chopping
Tourné knife	Cutting curved surfaces on vegetables

Other tools essential to a professional culinary kitchen include a rotary peeler, Parisienne scoop, kitchen fork, palette knife, wire whips, offset spatula, and pastry bag.

Measuring equipment includes graduated measuring pitchers, scales, thermometers, and measuring spoons. Sieves, strainers, and chinois are used mainly to sift, strain, aerate, and remove large impurities from dry ingredients.

A varied assortment of pots, pans, and molds are essential in the professional kitchen. (See Exhibit 3.) The most heat-efficient pots are made of either copper or cast iron. Because copper is expensive, often it is inserted within stainless steel, which offers easy maintenance at a lower cost. To select the right cooking utensils:

- Choose the size appropriate to the food being cooked.
- Choose material appropriate to the cooking technique.
- Use proper handling, cleaning, and storing procedures.

EXHIBIT 3—TYPES OF POTS, PANS, AND MOLDS

TYPE OF POT/PAN/MOLD	DESCRIPTION	USE
Stockpot (marmite)	Large pot, spigot	Stovetop cooking
Saucepot	Similar to stockpot; loop handles	Stovetop cooking
Saucepan	Slightly flared sides, long handle	Stovetop cooking
Rondeau (griswold)	Wide, shallow pot, two loop handles	Stovetop cooking
Sauteuse (sauté pan)	Shallow skillet, sloping sides, single long handle	Stovetop cooking
Sautoir (sauté pan)	Shallow skillet, straight sides, single long handle	Stovetop cooking
Omelet pan/crêpe pan	Shallow skillet, very short, slightly sloping sides	Stovetop cooking
Bain marie (double boiler)	Nesting pots with single long handles; bottom pot filled with water to gently cook food	Stovetop cooking

(continues page 9)

EXHIBIT 3—continued

TYPE OF POT/PAN/MOLD	DESCRIPTION	USE
Griddle	Flat, heavy round or rectangular surface	Stovetop cooking
Fish poacher	Long, narrow pot, straight sides, perforated rack	Stovetop cooking
Steamer	Set of stacked pots, upper pot has perforated bottom	Stovetop cooking
Wok, couscoussiére, paella pan, grill pan	Specialty pots and pans used for ethnic dishes	Stovetop cooking
Roasting pan	Rectangular pan, medium-high sides, various sizes	Oven roasting or baking
Sheet pan	Shallow, rectangular pan; full or half size	Oven baking
Pâté mold	Deep rectangular metal mold, hinged sides	Oven cooking/baking
Terrine mold	Rectangular or oval, with lid	Oven cooking/baking
Gratin dish	Shallow, oval ceramic dish	Oven cooking/baking
Soufflé	Round, straight-edged ceramic dish	Oven cooking/baking
Timbale mold	Small metal or ceramic mold, used for individual portions, usually vegetables	
Dariole, savarin, ring molds	Molds used to achieve varying shapes	

Large equipment must be properly maintained and used with extreme care, according to the manufacturer's safety regulations.

EXHIBIT 4—TYPES OF EQUIPMENT

TYPE OF EQUIPMENT	DESCRIPTION	USE
Meat grinder	Free-standing or attachment	Grinds meats to varying consistencies
Vertical chopping machine	Similar to a blender	Slices foods in even thicknesses
Food chopper	Rotating bowl passes under a hood where blades chop food	Chops food coarsely
Food processor		Grinds, ships, emulsifies, blends, or crushes food

(continues page 10)

EXHIBIT 4—continued

TYPE OF EQUIPMENT	DESCRIPTION	USE
Mandoline	Slicing machine	For julienne, arufrette, and batonnet
Steam-jacket kettle	Free-standing or tabletop unit circulates steam through the walls	For stocks, soups, sauces
Tilting kettle	Shallow, free-standing unit	For braising and stewing
Pressure steamer	Water heated under pressure at temperatures higher than boiling; automatic timer controls cooking time	Steams food quickly
Convection steamer	Steam vented evenly over food; less danger of burns than with pressure steamer	Steams food
Open-burner range	Grate-style burner, easy heat adjustment	Fast-order foods
Flat-top range	Gives even, consistent heat; heat not quickly adjustable	Heats and reheats food
Ring-top range	Flat-top with removable plates; easy to adjust heat	Fast-order foods
Convection oven	Hot air circulated via fans	Cooks food evenly, quickly
Conventional/deck oven	Heat source located on bottom	Used mostly for roasting
Griddle	Similar to a flat-top; food cooked directly on surface	Eggs, pancakes, and other to-order foods
Grill/broiler/salamander	Adjustable racks allow food to be raised and lowered to control cooking speed	Salamander used to finish or glaze foods
Walk-in refrigerator	Largest refrigeration unit with shelves around the walls; various foods can be stored in different temperature zones	Large space
Reach-in refrigerator	Available as single unit or part of a bank	Useful in pantry area
On-site refrigerator	Refrigerated drawers	Useful in holding foods online during service
Portable refrigerator	Refrigerated cart that can be moved as needed	Banquet and buffet preparation
Display refrigerator	Display cases	Used to show desserts, salads, or salad bars

Cooking Methods

Different cooking methods produce different results; therefore, it is important to pair the food with the appropriate cooking technique to obtain the desired results. There are three general categories of cooking methods: *dry heat-cooking*, with or without fat as a cooking medium; *moist-heat methods*, with liquid or steam as a cooking medium; and *combination methods*, using a combination of dry- and moist-heat. (See Exhibit 5.)

In the *dry-heat method*, food is cooked either by a direct application of radiant heat or by indirect heat contained in a closed environment. *Grilling* is a quick dry-heat technique that is excellent for cooking smaller pieces of food. The food is cooked over a radiant heat source. Barbecuing, broiling, and pan-broiling are forms of grilling. In *barbecuing*, the food has been basted with a sauce during grilling; in *broiling*, the heat source is located above the food item; *pan-broiled* meats are cooked on top of the stove in a heavy cast iron pan, with any fat or juices removed as the food is cooked.

Grilled foods have a smoky, slightly charred flavor which results from the flaring of the juices and fats that are rendered out as the food cooks. The use of special woods—mesquite, hickory, or apple—gives the food a distinct flavor. Marinating also gives meat a unique flavor. Crosshatch marks appear on the food's surface when the item is grilled properly. The grill racks must be perfectly clean to prevent foods from sticking or charring. Dividing the grill into zones helps the chef keep track of the items' doneness during a busy service period. The food must be turned, cooked, and finished to the desired doneness.

Indirect-heat methods of dry-heat cooking include roasting, barding, and smoke-roasting. Roasting is a technique that cooks foods by surrounding them with dry air in a closed environment. The air captured in the oven is the cooking medium, and the rendered juices are the foundation for sauces prepared while the roast rests. Roasted foods should have a golden-brown exterior and a tender, moist interior.

Spit-roasting, the oldest form of cookery, cooks food by radiant heat given off from a fire or other source. Food is placed on a rod that is turned either manually or with a motor. The constant turning assures that the food cooks evenly and develops a good crust. *Barding* is a term used for meats wrapped in thick sheets of fat. The meat will not have a well-developed or flavorful crust, as in grilling, but the interior will be more moist. *Smoke-roasting* allows foods to take on the rich, smoky flavor of hardwood chips without undergoing lengthy brining and smoking processes. The food is placed on a rack over smoldering hardwood chips, tightly covered, and roasted in a hot oven to the desired doneness.

Another way to prepare food is to use dry-heat cooking methods with fats and oils. These methods include sautéing, stir-frying, panfrying, and deep-frying. *Sautéing* and *stir-frying* use a small amount of oil, while *panfrying* uses a proportionately larger amount of oil and coating. Stir-fried foods should not appear raw and should have an appropriate color, with a moist and tender texture. Foods prepared in the panfrying technique are usually coated with batter or breaded and cooked in a larger amount of oil over less intense heat. The hot oil seals the food's coated surface and locks the natural juices inside, instead of releasing them.

Moist-heat cooking techniques produce foods that are delicately flavored and moist with a rich broth, which can be served as a separate course or as a sauce base. One technique is *steaming*, which is healthful as well as tasty. Food is placed in a closed vessel above the liquid. As the liquid comes to a boil, some of it turns to steam, which circulates around the food, providing an even, moist environment. The food retains most of its natural juices.

Steamed foods should be cooked until they are just done but not overcooked. Their flavor is delicate, and their appearance is usually pale because they are not browned. Steamed foods should be moist and plump, with no hint of rubberiness. They generally contain a greater proportion of nutrients because water-soluble nutrients are not drawn out of the food as readily. A flavorful liquid may be served as a broth or reduced as a sauce base.

In *poaching* and *simmering*, food is completely submerged in a liquid that is kept at a constant, moderate temperature. The poaching liquid must be well flavored, and the food selected should be naturally tender. The food is cooked at 180°F to 185°F (81°C to 82°C). The surface of the poaching liquid should show some motion, but no air bubbles should break the surface. Less tender items can be simmered because the food is cooked at a slightly higher temperature, 185°F to 200°F (82°C to 85°C). Simmered foods should never be boiled; the motion will cause food to become stringy and rubbery. Poached and simmered items are often served with a pungent sauce to add zest to the dish's mild flavor.

Combination cooking methods—braising and *stewing*—use both dry and moist heat to cook foods that are less tender. These are useful techniques for the professional chef because they require less tender and less expensive main ingredients; however, tender cuts also can be braised or stewed successfully. In *braising*, the item is seared in hot oil, slowly cooked in a small amount of liquid, and finished in the oven or on the stovetop until it is fork-tender (the food will slide easily from a kitchen fork inserted at the food's thickest part). Braising techniques include *daube, estouffade, pot roast,* and *swissing*.

In *stewing*, which is similar to braising, the main item is cut into bite-sized pieces. The amount of liquid used in relation to the amount of the item varies from one style of preparation to another. *Blanching*, which means to place the food in a pot of cold stock or water and bring the liquid to a boil, improves the color and flavor of the finished stew. Skimming the surface of the blanching liquid removes any impurities that could give a stew a gray color or off flavor.

Blanching is also an effective way to cook fried chicken. Food is cooked at a lower temperature and finished later by cooking in deep fat. The food cooks evenly but the crust is not completely brown. In finishing, the food is cooked to the proper color.

EXHIBIT 5—DRY AND MOIST HEAT COOKING METHODS

DRY HEAT WITHOUT FATS AND OILS	DRY HEAT WITH FATS AND OILS	MOIST HEAT
Grilling	Sautéing	Steaming
Broiling	Stir-frying	En papillote
Roasting	Panfrying	Shallow poaching
Poêléing	Deep-frying	Poaching
Smoke-roasting		Simmering
Spit-roasting		

Progress Check 1

Complete the following statements by writing the correct word or words in each blank. Check your answers against the answer key for Progress Check 1 on p. 59.

1. ____________________ occurs when disease-causing elements are transferred from one contaminated surface to another.

2. The ____________________ knife, smaller than the chef's knife, is used primarily for light cutting.

3. The potential to be a carrier of a foodborne illness is greater in foods that contain a high amount of ____________________.

4. The process of using moist heat or chemical agents to kill pathogenic micro-organisms is called ____________________.

5. The temperature range in which foods are most susceptible to contamination, called the temperature danger zone, is __________°F to __________°F.

6. ____________________, which are found in breads, grains, and pasta, are an important source of energy.

7. In the ____________________ method, food is cooked using a direct application of radiant heat or by indirect heat contained in a closed environment.

8. ____________________ techniques include shallow poaching, poaching, and simmering.

9. Roasting, barding, and smoke-roasting are ____________________ methods of dry-heat cooking.

10. Steamed foods should be ____________________ and ____________________, with no hint of rubberiness.

MEAT, POULTRY, AND SEAFOOD

Purchasing, Preparing, and Cooking Meat

For most foodservice operations, purchasing, preparing, and serving meats is one of the most expensive, yet potentially profitable, areas of business. The selection of any cut of meat is determined by the restaurant's menu. Made-to-order preparations require more tender cuts, while some cooking techniques can make use of less tender cuts. Other factors that influence a restaurant's meat purchases are storage space, available kitchen equipment, and the staff's ability to butcher large cuts of meat.

Meats and game should be loosely wrapped and stored under refrigeration, preferably in a separate unit. The chef should separate different types of meat to prevent cross-contamination. Meat stored at the proper temperature and under optimal conditions can be held for several days without a noticeable quality loss. While government inspection of meat is mandatory, grading is optional. The U.S. Department of Agriculture has established specific standards and trains graders. (See Exhibit 6.) Different grading terminology is used for all types of meat.

EXHIBIT 6—USDA QUALITY GRADES FOR MEATS

Mandatory inspection of meat and poultry shipped in interstate commerce

Voluntary grading for packers of meat and poultry

Voluntary inspection and grading for firms handling shell eggs

Meat

Meat

Wholesomeness

Poultry

Poultry

Quality

The first large cuts in butchering, called the *primal cuts*, are the leg, loin, rib, and shoulder. These are further broken down into smaller cuts—roasts, steaks, shanks, etc. *Market forms* of meat are those cuts that are ready for sale. The cuts may be primal cuts or already fabricated portions. (See Exhibit 7.)

EXHIBIT 7—RELATIONS OF MAJOR CARCASS DIVISIONS FOR BEEF, VEAL, LAMB, AND PORK

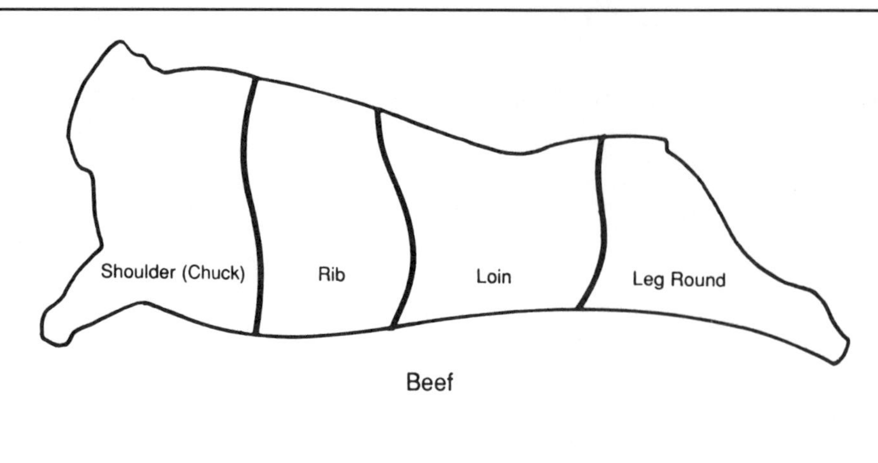

Beef

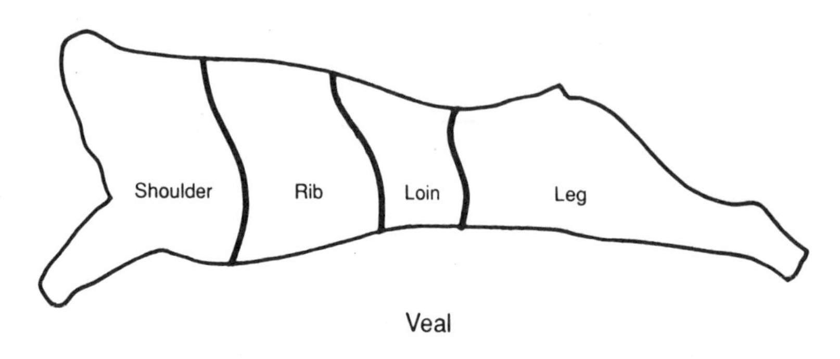

Veal

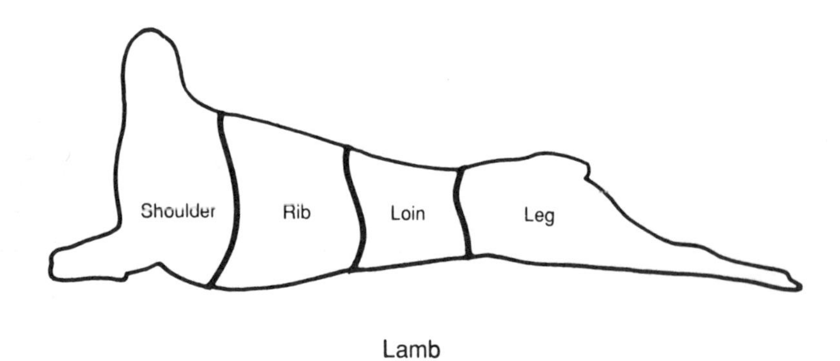

Lamb

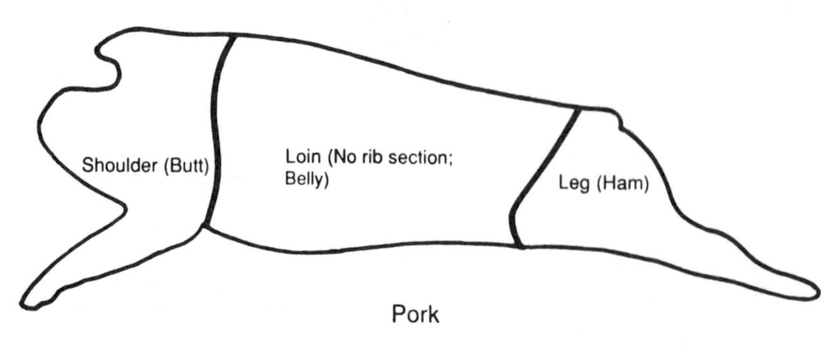

Pork

Reprinted with permission from The New Professional Chef, Fifth Edition, *by the Culinary Institute of America. Copyright © 1991 by Van Nostrand Reinhold.*

The amount of butchering necessary to prepare a market cut affects its price. Except for game, all market cuts of meat are assigned quality grades; beef and lamb have yield grades. The *yield grade* reflects the yield of usable meat after the fat has been trimmed.

Cattle that are butchered from the age of one day up to 14 to 15 weeks are sold as veal, a meat with a pale flesh and delicate flavor. The cuts are similar to those of beef. Veal or *offal* organ meats, especially sweetbreads, liver, calf's head, and brains appeal to patrons with gourmet palates.

Today, cuts of pork are leaner than those sold in the past. To prevent foodborne illnesses, pigs are slaughtered and butchered in facilities that handle no other type of meat.

Lamb has grown in popularity because the flavor of the meat has improved with better breeding methods. Sheep slaughtered under the age of one year are considered lamb; after that age they must be labeled *mutton*.

With the availability of game meats, including *fallow* or farm-raised deer, wild boar, and elk, the chef can prepare a variety of distinctly different dishes. The same general rules that determine proper cooking methods for red meat apply.

Kosher meats are specially slaughtered to comply with religious dietary laws. In the United States, only beef and veal forequarters, poultry, and some game are normally used for kosher preparations.

Fabrication means working with the primal cuts of meat to customize them to suit the menu and create specialty cuts that are not available from suppliers. Fabrication is essential in portion control and ensures that each portion's quality is always the same. Lean trim can be used to prepare au jus or stocks.

Fabrication techniques for meat (veal, lamb, pork, and large game are similar) involve practice and minimal equipment—essentially a sharp knife and a clean cutting board. The techniques include *tying* a roast, *trimming and boning* a pork loin, and *frenching* a rack of lamb.

A roast is frequently tied to ensure even cooking and retention of the meat's shape, and it is one of the easiest, most often used methods of meat fabrication.

Trimming a tenderloin must be done very carefully, especially since it is one of the most expensive cuts. The chef must be sure that only silverskin (the tough membrane), fat, and gristle are removed. First, the fat must be cut away. Then, a chef's knife is used to make an even cut through the center of the meat. Next, the meat is opened, and the chef has a cut that is thin enough to cook rapidly, which makes it an excellent choice for grilling or sautéing.

Frenching a rack of lamb is a complicated technique that requires practice. It is worthwhile for the chef to learn this procedure in preparing lamb, veal, or pork because frenching eliminates trim loss.

The meat is now ready to be made into a variety of menu cuts such as *medallions* (small medal-shaped pieces molded by wrapping them in cheesecloth); *noisettes* (little "nuts" of meat); *scallops* (thin, boneless cuts that are lightly pounded); and *émincé* (thin strips of meat, used for sautéing).

Meat can be prepared in a variety of ways, depending on the tenderness of the cut. Meats that are to be prepared by using one of the dry-heat methods—grilling, broiling, roasting, or poêléing—must be naturally tender or prepared in a way that will add moisture to make them more tender.

Determining doneness in foods prepared with the dry-heat methods is an imprecise science. Beef, lamb, and some game meats may be cooked to a range of doneness. Pressing the meat with the tip of a finger to gauge its resistance is one way to determine doneness. The less well-done a piece of meat is, the softer and more yielding it will feel. As the meat cooks, the exterior should develop a deep brown color. The more rare the meat, the bloodier the juices will appear. When the meat's upper surface begins to appear moist, the meat should be turned. White meats, such as veal and pork, should be cooked through but not overcooked. Thin meat pieces retain some heat, which allows them to continue cooking even when they have been removed from the heat source.

The sauce or gravy made from the drippings that accumulate during roasting is frequently referred to as *au jus*. When the jus made from drippings is thickened, it is known as *jus lié*. If a sauce is made with a roux incorporating the fat rendered from a roast, it is called *pan gravy*.

Carryover cooking describes what happens to a piece of meat after it has been removed from the oven. The roasted item holds a certain amount of heat that will continue to cook the food. The larger the item, the greater the amount of heat it will retain. A top round of beef's temperature may increase as much as 15°F and the temperature of a steamship round of beef by up to 20°F. The item should be removed from the oven when the internal temperature is lower than it should be when served.

Dry-heat cooking methods that use fats and oils cook meat in a brief amount of time, use high heat, and require tender, smaller pieces of meat. Sautéed meats are served with a sauce that is prepared while the food is cooking. The sauce is an important element because it captures the food's flavor lost during cooking, introduces additional flavor, and adds moisture. If meat strips are to be sautéed, the chef may choose to dust the item with flour.

In moist-heat cooking, meat is cooked in a liquid bath. An entire dinner, complete with vegetables, meat, fish, or poultry can be cooked in one pot.

Combination cooking methods, such as braising and stewing, require require less cooking liquid, a lower temperature, and a shorter cooking time.

When the meat is done cooking, let it rest before carving; prepare the gravy, and serve the roast with the gravy. Carve a rib roast with a sharp meat slicer, and use a knife tip to cut the slice away from the bone. A leg of lamb is carved by holding the shank bone firmly in one hand and making parallel cuts. Then cut slices of meat from the leg; when the slices become large, cut the meat at a slight angle.

Purchasing, Preparing, and Cooking Poultry

Poultry is becoming a standard menu item at most restaurants. Chicken is still the most popular form of poultry, but customer demand is increasing for squab, duck, quail, and pheasant. All types of poultry should be wrapped loosely and stored under refrigeration, and, where possible, stored in a separate unit or part of the cooler. To prevent cross-contamination, poultry should not come in contact with any other type of meat and should be placed on trays to prevent it from dripping on other foods or onto the floor. Since poultry has a short shelf life, it should be cooked as soon as possible after it is received.

Poultry is given a mandatory inspection for wholesomeness and may be graded as USDA A, B, or C. It is classified by size and age; the younger the bird, the more tender the flesh will be. Young fowl should have soft, smooth, pliable skin. The breast-bone cartilage should be flexible, as it is for domestic fowl. The flesh should be tender, with a slight "gamey" taste. The following factors determine its grade: shape of the carcass; ratio of meat to bone; freedom from pinfeathers, hair, and down; and number (if any) of tears, cuts, or broken bones.

Traditionally, chefs could obtain most game birds only during the hunting season; today many game birds are raised on farms year-round. However, many of these birds are still considered "wild" and are at their best from October through December or January.

A readily available food, poultry is less costly than other meats. When fabricated on the premises, the chef can get the best quality for the best possible price and have the valuable trim for stocks, soups, sauces, hors d'oeuvres, and forcemeats. Poultry fabrication includes disjointing and boning; creating suprêmes; cutting a bird into halves, quarters, and eighths; and trussing. This fabrication is easier than for other meats because the bird's bones are smaller and easier to cut through. The size and breed of a bird has some bearing on the ease of fabrication, but the methods are similar. Essential tools required for fabrication include a clean work surface, boning knife, and chef's knife.

To disjoint and bone poultry:

- Cut the legs away from the body.
- Cut the thigh and drumstick bones from the leg meat.
- Cut the breast away from the rib cage.

The breast is ready to be made into *suprêmes*:

- Cut away the first two wing joints. Use the heel of a chef's knife to cut the end of the remaining wing joint.
- Scrape the meat away from the wing bone, leaving as little meat as possible on the bone.
- Cut the meat away from the wing bone.

Cutting poultry into halves, quarters, and eighths is a useful technique for small and large birds alike. The size of the cut depends on the size of the bird, and the method of cooking.

Sanitation rules must be strictly observed in poultry fabrication to prevent cross-contamination:

- Poultry should be refrigerated between 32°F and 36°F when it is not being fabricated.
- Clean and sanitize the cutting board and all cutting utensils before and after fabrication.
- Store poultry in clean, leak-proof containers.
- Never place poultry above cooked meats.

Trussing, or tying poultry, gives the bird a smooth, compact shape that ensures even cooking and moisture retention.

Once the poultry has been properly fabricated, a variety of cooking methods is available. Poultry is especially suited to the dry-heat cooking techniques of grilling and broiling, roasting, and poêléing. As with grilling beef, the grill or broiler should be mentally divided into zones to keep track of the items' doneness. The chef should also identify which grill areas tend to be hotter than others. Chicken and other poultry should be cooked through, but not overcooked, and there should be a slight amount of "give" when the meat is pressed with a fingertip. Any juices should be nearly colorless.

Roasting and *poêléing* (or butter roasting) require longer cooking times because these techniques are most frequently used with whole birds. To roast a whole bird, the item should be seasoned, stuffed, marinated, barded, or larded and seared over direct heat or in a hot oven if desired. The bird should be elevated in a roasting pan so that hot air can reach all sides, and roasted uncovered until the desired internal temperature is reached. Poultry should be cooked until well-done, or 150°F to 165°F (65°C to 72°C). The skin should be crisp, creating a contrast with the meat's texture.

Of the two techniques, poêléing is most often associated with game birds and chicken. Meats are allowed to cook in their own juices in a covered vessel on a bed of aromatic vegetables, or *matignon*, which then becomes a garnish served as part of the sauce.

Chicken and poultry are also well suited to dry-heat cooking with fats and oils: sautéing, stir-frying, panfrying, and deep-frying. These techniques require tender, portion-size pieces.

Stir-frying is another technique especially suited to chicken. Since the chicken is cut into small pieces, which acts as a means of tenderizing the food, the pieces do not need to be as naturally tender as for sautés. A variety of foods may be combined in this method, but whatever the main item is, it should be carefully trimmed and cut into regular pieces. Marinated chicken should be patted dry before adding it to the cooking oil.

A very popular method for preparing chicken is deep-frying. Foods prepared by deep-frying are breaded or batter coated and cooked by being completely submerged in hot fat. The result is an interesting combination of flavors and textures. Chicken that is deep-fried must be naturally tender. The swimming, basket, and double-basket methods are variations of deep-fat cooking. In the *swimming method*, batter-coated foods are gently dropped in the hot oil, fall to the bottom of the fryer, then float to the surface. Foods cooked in the *basket method* are breaded, lowered into the hot oil, and then lifted out in the basket when they are done. The *double-basket technique* is used for certain foods that need to be fully submerged in hot oil for a longer period of time to develop a crisp crust.

The amount of time it takes the oil to return to the correct temperature after a product has been cooked is the *recovery time*. The more food items that are cooked in the oil, the longer the recovery time.

The *smoking point* is the temperature at which fats and oils begin to smoke, a condition that indicates that the fat has begun to break down. Oils used for deep-frying should have a neutral flavor and color, and a high smoking point (around 425°F or 218°C).

Most deep-fried foods are done when the items have risen to the surface and they appear golden-brown. One exception is tempura-dipped foods, which will be light gold. The crust should be crisp and delicate, encasing a moist, tender piece of poultry (meat or fish).

Steaming is a healthful way to prepare poultry. Steamed poultry should take on an evenly opaque appearance and the flesh should offer little resistance when pressed with a fingertip.

Chicken is a natural for combination cooking methods of stewing and braising. A properly prepared braise or stew is a dish of complexity and flavor concentration that is not possible with other cooking techniques. The sauce has exceptional body, and the proteins and other nutrients lost from the main item into the cooking liquid are not lost to the dish itself.

To carve any type of poultry, use one kitchen fork to hold the breast steady, and use a knife tip to cut through the skin at the point where the leg meets the breast. Insert another kitchen fork between the drumstick and the thigh. Pull the leg away from the body. Repeat this process for the other leg. Cut the leg into two pieces. Then, cut through the breast's skin on either side of the breastbone to remove the meat. Use a kitchen fork to gently pull the breast meat away from the rib cage and cut the breast meat completely away with a knife tip.

Purchasing, Preparing, and Cooking Seafood

Only the freshest fish should be purchased and then prepared in a manner that highlights the particular taste of the fish. Following are ways to determine freshness and quality:

- The fish should have a fresh, clean "sea" aroma.
- The skin should feel slick and moist.
- The fins and tail should be moist, fresh, flexible, and full.
- The flesh should feel firm and elastic.
- The eyes should be clear and full, and the gills should have a red or maroon color.
- Live crab and lobster should move about; clams, mussels, and oysters should be tightly closed.

If any of the criteria are not met, the fish should be rejected.

Ideally, the chef should purchase the amount of fish needed for one or two days. If daily deliveries are not possible, here are some tips for properly storing fish and seafood for several days:

- Check the fish carefully for freshness and quality.
- Place the fish on a bed of shaved or flaked ice in a perforated container.
- Cover with additional ice.
- Set the perforated container inside a second container.
- Thoroughly drain and re-ice fish daily until used. In addition, there are special ways to properly store clams, mussels, scallops, and live shellfish.

Market cuts of fish and seafood include:

- Whole or round fish—the fish as it was caught
- Drawn fish—viscera (internal organs) removed
- Dressed fish—viscera, scales, and fins removed
- Steaks—cross-section cuts, generally from large fish

- Fillets—boneless sides of fish
- Shucked—refers to the removal of a mollusk or fish from its shell

There are three basic categories of fish—*round fish* (trout, bass, perch); *flat fish* (flounder, sole); and *nonbony fish* (ray, shark, monkfish). Within these broad categories are a wide range of flavors and textures. When the chef fabricates fish, every bit of trim can be put to use in a mousseline, a filling, canapés, soups, or sauce. Fish fabrication techniques consist of scaling, trimming, gutting, and filleting. Scaling methods are the same for both round and flat fish, but procedures differ slightly for gutting and filleting. The tools needed for fabrication are a sharp, flexible filleting knife, needlenose pliers, and a clam and oyster knife.

Filleting is the most common technique of fish fabrication. Boneless, skinless pieces can be sautéed, grilled, baked, or formed into a variety of special shapes.

Once the fish has been filleted, it can be made into various cuts, such as *goujonettes* (small strips); *paupiettes* (thin, rolled fillets, filled with stuffing); and *steaks*.

Shellfish are cleaned by removing the shell and vein or intestine. Sometimes the fish is returned to the shell for an attractive presentation. Shrimp are usually peeled and deveined. Shrimp that has been boiled or steamed in its shell will be moister and plumper than shrimp that has been peeled and deveined before cooking. Crayfish can be cleaned in the same manner as shrimp. The vein and intestine must be removed.

When working with lobster, it is easier to remove the meat from the shell when the lobster has been partially or fully cooked. Blanching the lobster lightly in a steam bath, in boiling water, or in a hot oven is all that is required to firm the flesh enough to remove it cleanly from the shell.

Since clams and oysters are often served on the half shell, it is important not to destroy the shell when removing the flesh. All mollusks should be scrubbed well with a brush under cold, running water before being opened.

The best way to pair a fish with a cooking technique is to consider the flesh. For example, mackerel, an oily fish, cooks best with a dry-heat technique, such as grilling or broiling. Tuna or salmon, which contain a moderate amount of fat, can be prepared using any cooking method. Very lean fish, such as sole and flounder, are most flavorful when they are poached or sautéed.

Moist-heat cooking techniques and combination cooking methods are very effective for cooking fish. One moist-heat cooking technique that is especially suitable to fish is *en papillote*. In this method of steaming, the main ingredient (resting on a bed of herbs, vegetables, or sauce) and accompanying items are encased in parchment paper and cooked in a hot oven. As in the steaming method, the liquid vapor created by the food's natural juices cooks the food. Fish cooked en papillote is done when the bag is very puffy and the paper is brown.

Shallow poaching is another method suitable for fish. This method cooks foods using a combination of steam and a liquid bath: the food is partially submerged in a liquid that often contains an acid, such as wine or lemon juice, and aromatics, such as shallots and herbs. The cooking vessel is covered to capture some of the steam released by the liquid during cooking; the captured steam cooks the portion of the food not directly in the liquid.

In shallow poaching, a significant amount of flavor is transferred between the food and the liquid. To retain the flavor released into the liquid, the liquid is reduced and used as a sauce base. Fish fillets are suitable because they are naturally tender and delicate.

Shallow-poached foods should be cooked until they are just done. Fish and shellfish should be opaque; the flesh of oysters, clams, and mussels should show curling on the edges.

Fish should be opaque, with a delicate color appropriate to the type. For example, turbot should be very white; salmon should be a delicate pink or orange-pink color. The finished item should be moist and extremely tender. Any stringiness, dryness, or excessive flaking indicates that the food was cooked too long or at too high a temperature.

Combination cooking methods of stewing and braising have produced some very popular fish recipes over the years, such as Bouillabaisse, shrimp jambalaya, and seafood Newburg.

Charcuterie and Garde-manger

The art of *charcuterie* dates back to the Middle Ages, and now includes the preparation of pork and other meat items such as hams, terrines, and forcemeats. *Garde-manger* refers to the preparation of cold foods, including salads, pâtés, and appetizers. A basic component of charcuterie and garde-manger items is *forcemeat*—a lean meat and fat emulsion with either a coarse or smooth consistency formed when the ingredients are forced through a sieve or grinder. Certain guidelines must be followed during the preparation of forcemeats:

- Proper sanitation and temperature must be observed at all times. The ingredients (pork, poultry, seafood, and dairy products) are classified as potentially hazardous foods and must be kept at temperatures below 40°F (4°C).
- Foods must be ground properly. Cut all foods into dices or strips that will fit easily into the grinder. Be sure the blade is sharp.

Progress Check 2

Complete the following statements by writing the correct word or words in each blank. Check your answers against the answer key for Progress Check 2 on p. 59.

1. The beef ____________ contains four primal cuts: rib, chuck (shoulder), brisket, and foreshank; the ____________ contains two primal cuts: the loin and the leg.

2. The most expensive and tender cut of beef is the ____________.

3. Sweetbreads are considered ____________ meats.

4. ____________ is a collection of basic techniques used to customize primal cuts and ensure portion and quality control.

5. The ____________ reflects the field of usable meat after the fat has been trimmed.

6. ____________ is sauce or gravy made from accumulated meat drippings.

7. Fish prepared ____________ are considered done when the bag is fluffy and the paper is brown.

8. ____________ are cleaned by removing the shell and vein or intestine.

9. Poultry should be cooked until ____________, or to between 150°F and 165°F.

10. The three basic categories of fish are ____________, ____________, and ____________.

STOCKS, SOUPS, AND SAUCES

Preparing Stocks

Stocks are the chef's building blocks because they form the base for many soups and sauces. A *stock* is a flavorful liquid made by gently simmering bones or vegetables in a liquid to extract their flavor, aroma, color, body, and nutrients. All stocks contain four essential components: a major flavoring ingredient, liquid, aromatics, and mirepoix. The taste of a stock should be easily identified but not so strong that it overpowers the other ingredients used in the finished dish. Fish, chicken, and beef stock have the strongest flavors; white veal stock is considered neutral. There are several types of stock:

- *White stock* is a clear, colorless liquid made by simmering poultry, beef, or fish bones.
- *Brown stock* is an amber liquid made by first browning poultry, beef, veal, or game bones.
- *Fumet* is a highly flavored stock made with fish bones.
- *Court bouillon* is an aromatic vegetable broth.
- *Essence* is the same as fumet, but with highly aromatic vegetables.
- *Glacé*, or glaze, is a reduced stock that develops a jellylike consistency.
- *Remouillage* is a stock made from bones that have already been used in another preparation. It can replace water as the liquid requirement in stock.
- *Broth* or *bouillon* is the liquid that results from simmering meats.

The *mise en place* (the preparation and assembly of ingredients, pans, utensils, and plates or serving pieces needed for a recipe) for stock consists of several items:

1. Major flavoring ingredient, usually bones and trimmings for meat or fish stocks. Vegetables are used for vegetable essences and court bouillons.
2. Water is the liquid most frequently used. If remouillage is substituted, it will produce a richly flavored stock. The ratio of liquid to flavoring ingredients is standard:
    - Chicken, beef, veal, and game stock: 8 pounds of bones to 6 quarts of water yield 1 gallon of stock. One pound of mirepoix is needed.
    - Fish/shellfish stock or fumet: 11 pounds of bones or shells to 5 quarts of water and 1 pound of mirepoix yield 1 gallon.
    - Vegetable essences: 1 pound of vegetables to 1 quart of water.

3. *Mirepoix* (a combination of chopped aromatic vegetables used for flavoring) should be trimmed and cut into a size appropriate for the type of stock.

4. Aromatics should include either a standard sachet d'epices or bouquet garni. If salt is added, it should be used sparingly.

The bones used must be cut into the right size and prepared by blanching, browning, or sweating. The bones or shells used in fumets must be sweated, a process in which bones and mirepoix are gently cooked before the liquid is added. Fish bones and shellfish can take on an unpleasant flavor if they are cooked too long. The sweating process releases the flavor quickly, in less than 45 minutes.

Stocks are evaluated on the basis of their flavor, color, aroma, and clarity. The major flavoring ingredient should dominate, and it should taste fresh. With the exception of vegetable essences and fumet, stocks should be almost crystal clear when they are hot. A high-quality stock may take up to eight hours to properly cook; however, it is the most cost effective, flavorful way to use valuable meat and fish trim.

If a stock must be absolutely clear, it is possible to clarify it by combining 1 gallon of cold stock with four beaten egg whites, then bringing the stock to a simmer. The egg whites trap the impurities and are skimmed away. This procedure should be done only when absolutely necessary because it weakens the stock's flavor.

Preparing Soups

Any good soup is made with the best ingredients available. There are two kinds of soup: *clear soups* and *thick soups.* (See Exhibit 8.) Flavored stocks and broths are considered clear soups; cream soups, purée soups, and bisques are considered thick soups. Major flavoring components must be carefully selected. Meats should be flavorful; cuts from the neck, hocks, or short ribs are preferred. Stewing hens are the best choice for chicken soups; fish and shellfish must be fresh; vegetables should also be fresh and savory. Mirepoix, sachet d'epices, and bouquet garni contribute flavor.

Most soups are cooked at a gentle simmer and stirred occasionally. Any scum or foam should be removed with a skimmer. It is a mistake to overcook soup—not only does the flavor become flat, but all the nutrients are exhausted.

Techniques for cooling and finishing are essential. Clear soups should be garnished just before serving. Cream soups should have the cream added just before service and not be allowed to boil. Final seasonings should be added after the soup is finished. Only the amount of soup that is to be used for the service should be reheated. Clear soups should be brought to a full boil, while thick soups should be reheated gently. Soups can be microwaved if they are placed in microwave-safe bowls, stirred, and returned to the microwave before serving.

Following are some tips for preparing soups:

- To bolster the flavor of a weak broth or consommé, a meat or poultry glaze may be added.
- Chopped fresh herbs, lemon juice, or a dash of Tabasco sauce can brighten a soup's flavor.
- Light sprinklings of salt and pepper can be added just before service.
- Remove surface fat on soup before service. Blot the soup with strips of unwaxed brown butcher paper floating on the surface.
- Garnish soups just before serving.
- The best way to clarify beef broth that has become cloudy is to add egg whites.

EXHIBIT 8—SOUP FORMULAS

Following are standard formulas for broth, consommé, and cream soups. From these formulas, the chef can create vegetable soup, cream of chicken soup, and others.

Basic Broth Formula

- Combine the meat and stock.
- Bring to an even simmer.
- Add the mirepoix and bouquet garni.
- Simmer to the appropriate cooking times depending on the main ingredient: beef, veal, game, chicken—2 to 3 hours; fish—30 to 40 minutes; vegetables—30 minutes to one hour.
- Skim; strain; cool and store, or finish and garnish for service.

A good broth should be clear, pale amber, with the distinct flavor of the major ingredient.

Basic Consommé Formula

- Combine the ground meat, mirepoix, seasonings, tomato product, oignon brûlé (peeled, halved onion, seared for flavoring), and egg white.
- Blend in the stock.
- Bring to a boil.
- Stir frequently.
- Simmer.
- Do not stir after the raft (the meat and egg white proteins that rise to the surface) has formed.
- Break a hole in the raft.
- Simmer until the consommé has developed flavor, body, and color.
- Strain; cool and store, or finish and garnish for service.

Good consommé should be crystal clear, aromatic, and emphasize the flavor of the major ingredient.

(continues page 29)

EXHIBIT 8—continued

Basic Cream Soup Formula

- Sweat the vegetables in fat or stock.
- Add the flour and cook out the roux.
- Add the liquid.
- Bring to a boil.
- Lower to a simmer.
- Add the bouquet garni or sachet d'épices and the main ingredient.
- Skim; discard the bouquet garni or sachet d'épices as necessary.
- Strain; purée the solids.
- Reincorporate the liquid to the proper consistency.
- Strain; cool and store, or finish with cream and garnish for service.

The major ingredient in cream soups should dominate, and there should be no strong flavor of cream.

Purée soups are slightly thicker than cream soups, with a coarser texture. To keep this consistency, the major flavoring ingredients and aromatics are strained out of the cooked soup and puréed separately.

Bisques are another variation of cream and purée soups. They are based on shrimp, lobster, or crayfish puréed to enhance the flavor of the major ingredient, making the texture slightly grainy. A properly prepared bisque should emphasize the flavor of the crustacean, and have a pale pink or red color.

Specialty or national soups include minestrone, chowders, and gumbos. There are also cold soups such as vichyssoise, cantaloupe soup, and gazpacho. Their addition to the menu depends on availability and customer preference.

Preparing Sauces

There are two major categories of sauces—grand sauces and contemporary sauces. The *grand sauces* include brown or demi-glacé, velouté, béchamel, tomato, and hollandaise. Although their use has diminished over the years, they still retain an important role in professional kitchens. *Contemporary sauces* often take less time to prepare, can be updated versions of grand sauces, and usually are lighter in color and body.

Excellent *demi-glacé* has a full, rich flavor, deep brown color, and evenly coats the back of a spoon (known as *nappé*). A top layer of clarified butter will prevent a skin from forming as the sauce is being held for service.

Velouté, based on chicken, veal, or fish stock, is prepared by thickening a white stock with an appropriate amount of pale roux, then simmering it until the roux contains no lumps. Velouté is commonly used in the preparation of cream soups.

Béchamel is a white sauce made by thickening milk with a white roux and simmering it with aromatics. It should have a creamy flavor, a definite sheen, and absolutely no graininess.

Properly prepared *tomato sauce* has a deep, rich tomato flavor, opaque color, and a little coarser texture than the other grand sauces.

Hollandaise is an emulsion sauce that is formed when melted or clarified butter is suspended in partially cooked egg yolks. It is a fragile sauce because unlike the other grand sauces, an emulsion is not a true mixture, and the sauce can break down.

During service, hollandaise must be held over a warm water bath, not a steam table, to keep it from breaking down. Properly prepared hollandaise will be a pale lemon color with a buttery flavor and frothy texture.

Jus and *jus lié* are contemporary sauces. *Jus lié* is a thickened sauce usually made from brown veal stock and can be used as a deglazer. Jus lié should have the full flavor of the major ingredient with no evidence of scorching.

In *beurre blanc*, butter forms an emulsion with a small reduction, resulting in a very fragile sauce. A small amount of heavy cream can stabilize the sauce so that it may be held during service. Beurre blanc has a creamy color, frothy texture, and buttery flavor.

Compound butters are used to finish grilled or broiled meats, fish, poultry, game, pastas, and sauces. Sometimes vegetables are tossed in compound butters before serving. The ingredients used in compound butters vary—herbs, nuts, citrus zest, shallots, ginger, and vegetables. Whole, unsalted butter, softened to room temperature, is blended with the appropriate seasoning. The butter is rolled into a cylinder in parchment paper and thoroughly chilled.

Progress Check 3

Complete the following statements by writing the correct word or words in each blank. Check your answers against the answer key for Progress Check 3 answers on p. 59.

1. ______________________ is an emulsion sauce that is formed when clarified butter is suspended in partially cooked egg yolks.

2. The five grand, or mother, sauces are ______________________, ______________________, ______________________, ______________________, and ______________________.

3. ______________________ soups may be degreased by floating unwaxed brown butcher paper on the top before serving.

4. An ______________________ is formed when one substance is suspended within another.

5. ______________________ is a process that removes some or all of the water in a liquid and concentrates the flavor.

6. ______________________ is a prepared mixture containing equal parts of flour and fat used to thicken liquids.

7. A highly flavored stock made with fish bones is called ______________________.

8. ______________________ is a thickened sauce, usually made from brown veal stock.

9. ______________________ or ______________________, is a reduced stock that develops a jellylike consistency.

10. There are two kinds of soups: ______________________ soups and ______________________ soups.

FRUITS, VEGETABLES, HERBS, GRAINS, AND NONPERISHABLE FOODS

Purchasing, Preparing, and Cooking Fruits and Vegetables

The role of fruits, vegetables, and herbs in a well-balanced diet is even more important today as nutrition-conscious consumers seek to maintain healthier lifestyles. As with any food, the professional chef must be able to select fruits, vegetables, and herbs that are of the quality most appropriate for the intended use.

What constitutes a fresh appearance varies from one item to another; however, there are some common traits. Fruits and vegetables should be free of bruises, mold, brown or soft spots, and pest damage. The color and texture should be appropriate to the particular type of fruit or vegetable, and any attached leaves should be unwilted. Fruits should be plump, never shriveled. The USDA has developed a grading system; however, lower graded items, particularly fruits, can be successfully used in dishes such as baked pies, puddings, and cobblers where their appearance is not a factor.

All produce must be properly stored, with ripe fruits and vegetables (except for bananas, potatoes, and dry onions) kept under refrigeration at a temperature of 40°F–45°F (4°C–7°C), with a relative humidity of 80–90 percent. Whenever possible, fruits should be stored separately in one refrigerator, and vegetables stored in another unit. In addition, dairy products are very susceptible to absorbing food odors. Some produce such as onions or garlic give off odors that would taint the natural, delicate flavor of the dairy items.

Even with proper storage, most foodservice operations do not keep produce for more than four days. Some vegetables and citrus fruits have a longer life, but most restaurants limit the storage of these items to three weeks.

Herbs, the leaves of aromatic plants, should be used to enhance, not overwhelm, the flavor of foods. Most herbs are available both fresh and dry. Fresh herbs should be stored in a damp, loosely wrapped towel at 35°F–40°F (2°C–7°C) and should be cut as close to serving time as possible.

During cooking, fresh herbs are added toward the end of the cooking process, and dried herbs are added in the beginning. In uncooked dishes, fresh herbs should be among the first ingredients, to give them time to blend with other flavors.

Certain factors are essential in the successful preparation of vegetables. An operation should always purchase vegetables that are at the peak of quality, maintain proper storage and handling standards, and select a cooking process best suited to the vegetable. Vegetables must be cooked in a way that retains their nutritive value, best color, and freshest flavor.

Each vegetable cookery technique produces a different result. Methods such as stir-frying, microwaving, and steaming are often used for cooking vegetables that should have a crisp texture and bright color; boiled vegetables are more moist and tender; baking vegetables makes them fluffy with a unique roasted flavor. One way for the chef to add variety to a particular vegetable is to pair it with a technique not commonly used. For example, cucumbers are most often served raw, but when they are steamed, sautéed, or braised, the color, texture, and flavor are distinctly different.

The best overall quality is generally assured by cooking vegetables rapidly and serving them as soon as possible. Once any vegetable has been harvested, it begins to deteriorate. Sweet corn or peas begin to lose their quality, flavor, and texture almost from the moment they are picked. Root vegetables, however, lose their quality so slowly that they can be stored for months.

Vegetables must be properly prepared before they are cooked by any method. These preliminary preparations include peeling, cleaning, and slicing. Not all vegetables require peeling before cooking; however, for those that do require peeling, the chef should use either a rotary peeler or a paring knife to remove the skin evenly and neatly without removing the flesh.

Four factors determine how tender a vegetable should be cooked: the natural characteristics of the vegetable in its raw state; the quality standard for a particular cooking method; regional preferences; and characteristics of the particular vegetable when it is properly cooked. Appearance and texture are two tests of a vegetable's doneness. Green vegetables demonstrate a marked visual difference from one stage of doneness to the next. White and orange vegetables display very little color change, so their texture must be checked.

While there is no way to retain all of a vegetable's nutrients during the cooking process, there are ways to minimize their loss:

- Avoid holding vegetables in liquid before or after cooking.
- Rinse, trim, peel, and cut vegetables as close to cooking time as possible.
- Cook vegetables as quickly as possible, in as little liquid as possible.
- Cook vegetables as close to service time as possible.
- Steam, microwave, or bake vegetables whole, in their skins whenever possible.

Flavor retention depends on both the type of vegetable and the cooking method used. Methods of cooking vegetables include boiling, steaming, microwaving, roasting and baking, sautéing and stir-frying, panfrying, deep-frying, stewing and braising, and puréeing.

Steaming is an excellent way to prepare vegetables for to-order service and also the best method for retaining vitamins and minerals because they are cooked gently in a vapor bath, not in direct contact with water.

In the microwaving process, the friction of the vibrating food molecules generates heat, causing the food's natural liquids to steam the item. Vegetables can be cooked in an appropriate microwave-safe container with a small amount of liquid and covered; or the vegetable can be left whole, with skin or peel intact, and steamed with its own moisture.

When a vegetable is roasted or baked, it is generally left whole or cut into large pieces, with no additional liquid added. This technique is best suited to vegetables with thick skins that protect the interior from drying or scorching, such as winter squashes, potatoes, and eggplant.

Sautéing and stir-frying techniques give vegetables a crisp texture. Some vegetables are suitable for sautéing and stir-frying from their raw state, such as mushrooms and onions, while denser vegetables, such as green beans and carrots, must be partially cooked before they are sautéed or stir-fried. Cooked vegetables can be reheated by sautéeing prior to serving. This is called *finishing in butter. Glazing* is another finishing technique in which a small amount of honey, sugar, or maple syrup is added to the vegetable, coating it and giving it a sheen as it reheats. When vegetables are panfryed, they are often coated with breading or batter.

Vegetables that are to be deep-fried must be precooked. For best results, the vegetable should be coated with breading or batter just before cooking.

Some vegetables can be grilled or broiled from the raw state, while others require preliminary cooking or marinating. Vegetables prepared by grilling must be able to withstand the grill's intense heat. In some cases, the core or seeds should be removed and the cavity filled with a stuffing. Popular examples include broiled stuffed artichokes and stuffed tomatoes.

Vegetable stews and braises are good ways to retain the vitamins and minerals that are transferred to the cooking liquid because the liquid is served as part of the dish. Stewed vegetables are cut into small pieces, whereas braised vegetables are cut in large pieces or left whole.

Puréed vegetables can be served as individual dishes or may be used in other preparations, such as timbales, custards, or soufflés. It is essential that the vegetable be cooked until it is tender enough to purée easily by pushing it through a sieve or food mill, or by puréeing it in a vertical chopping machine or blender. Some vegetables, such as tomatoes, spinach, and cucumbers, can be puréed from the raw state.

Preparing and Cooking Potatoes, Grains, and Pasta

The potato is one of the most popular vegetables because of its versatility and wide appeal. A wide range of cooking techniques, including boiling, steaming, baking, sautéing, en casserole, deep-frying, and puréeing, can be applied to produce a number of preparations with special flavors, textures, and appearances. Different potato varieties will produce different results.

Potato varieties differ in starch and moisture content, shape, and skin color, with different varieties producing different results. The starch content of any potato increases with age. Sweet potatoes and yams share some characteristics with potatoes. *Idaho*, or *russet*, potatoes are suited to baking, pureeing, or frying because they are high in starch and low in moisture. *Chef's potatoes* are considered all-purpose potatoes because they contain moderate amounts of starch and moisture, and hold their shape even after they are cooked until tender. This makes them excellent choices for salads, scalloped or casserole dishes, soups, braising, and sautéing. *New potatoes* refer to any potato harvested when it is very small, less than 2 inches in diameter. New potatoes do not have to be peeled; they are high in moisture and low in starch.

Whenever possible, potatoes should be cooked in their skins to retain nutrients. Puréed potatoes must be peeled before cooking so that as little heat as possible is lost before they are puréed. Green spots, eyes, and sprouts should be completely removed because they contain a toxin that is harmful when eaten in large quantities. To prevent the discoloration that occurs rapidly after potatoes have been peeled or cut, submerge them in a liquid.

Boiled potatoes can be held for up to an hour covered loosely with a damp, clean cloth and kept warm. It is best to start boiling potatoes in cold water. Steaming is the best way to cook new potatoes and other varieties with a high moisture content. Steamed potatoes can be held for short periods in the same manner as boiled potatoes.

Baked potatoes are served in their skins, accompanied by a garnish. A variation of this method is oven-roasting potatoes in which the parcooked potato is browned and glazed with the drippings of a meat or poultry roast as it cooks in the oven. The potato should not be wrapped in foil prior to baking because the foil prevents the skin from becoming crisp. A properly baked potato has a crisp skin, with a fluffy, tender interior. Baked potatoes *should* be served immediately, but they can be held for less than an hour in a warm place.

En casserole potato dishes combine peeled, raw potatoes with heavy cream, sauce, or uncooked custard and are slowly baked. An especially creamy texture, without curdling, can be obtained by baking the potatoes in a bain-marie in the oven. These potatoes are well suited to banquet service because they are cut into portions easily and can be held in a warm place for a reasonable amount of time without losing quality.

Another popular method of cooking potatoes is deep-frying. Russet potatoes are best suited for deep-frying because of their low moisture content. Most potatoes prepared in deep-fat should be blanched to assure even cooking without a greasy, scorched flavor. Deep-fried potatoes cannot be held and should be served immediately.

Puréed potatoes are first boiled, steamed, or baked before they are combined with other ingredients or mashed. Whipped or mashed potatoes may be held for service in a bain-marie or steam table. Puréed potatoes that are to be used in other dishes may be held under refrigeration for several hours, but once the final cooking process is completed, they must be served at once.

Grains are a concentrated source of nutrients and fiber. Even more important, they are good-tasting, inexpensive, readily available, and provide a concentrated source of nutrients and fiber. *Legumes* grow in pods and are used either fresh or dried. They are important for their high protein content.

The purpose of cooking grains and legumes is to change their textures so they can be chewed and digested easily; to develop their flavor; and to deactivate certain natural substances that can be harmful to humans. They must be stored in a dry area, away from moisture, light, and excessive heat. Legumes will develop mold if they are stored under damp conditions.

Grains and legumes must be rinsed carefully and, in some cases, soaked before cooking. Then they should be placed in a large pot with cold water. Any grains or legumes that float on the surface should be discarded.

Soaking is not essential but it does shorten cooking time. When whole grains such as barley and buckwheat are soaked, the water softens the outer layer or *bran*. Legumes' tough seed coats do not absorb water quickly and may not become soft even after cooking. They can be soaked overnight in cold water or by using a quick method in which the legumes are boiled briefly and then soaked in the hot water for one hour.

Grains should not be held long after cooking. Pilafs should be prepared in batches throughout the service period. Cooked legumes may be held for a few days after cooking if they are cooled and stored under refrigeration in their cooking liquid.

There are several ways to cook grains, including boiling, steaming, pilaf, and risotto. Legumes can only be boiled. Grains are done when they are tender to the bite; legumes are done when they are very tender, with no hard core at the center.

Steamed grains are cooked in a double boiler with a perforated bottom. Properly steamed grains should be tender to the bite.

In the *pilaf method*, the grain is first heated in a pan, either dry or with oil, and then combined with hot liquid and cooked, covered, in the oven or on the stove top. The grains remain separate and have a nutty flavor.

The *risotto method* is usually used for one special short grain rice, arborio. The rice is stirred constantly as small amounts of hot liquid are added and absorbed by the grain. The rice's starch is released gradually during the cooking process, producing a creamy texture. The best risotto has a porridge-like consistency, and can be served as an appetizer or main entrée.

Pasta and dumplings have been important elements of most cuisines partly because they are made from inexpensive, staple ingredients and also because they adapt well to a number of uses—appetizers, entrées, salads, and even desserts. *Pasta* and *dumplings* are prepared from a dough or batter that always includes a starch, such as flour, meal, or potatoes, and a liquid. Additional ingredients may be added to change the dish's shape, color, texture, and flavor. The basic pasta dough recipe produces a stiff dough that can be stretched, rolled into thin sheets, and cut into desired shapes. Slight additions or changes can transform it into a dumpling batter for spatzli or breadlike dumplings used in stews.

Dumplings can be cooked in a variety of ways, depending on their type—simmered in liquid, steamed, poached, baked, pan- or deep-fried. Simmered or poached dumplings are quite popular. The only reliable test of a dumpling's doneness is to cut into one of them to be sure it does not have a doughy, uncooked interior.

Dried and fresh pasta each have their own advantages and disadvantages. Fresh pasta gives the chef more freedom to create unique dishes and cooks quickly, but it has a limited shelf life; dried pasta has a more pronounced "bite," an indefinite shelf life, but takes longer to cook.

There are three basic ways to mix pasta dough: by hand, in a food processor, or in an electric mixer. In all methods, the resting stage is the most important. If the dough is not sufficiently relaxed, it will be difficult to roll into thin sheets. When vegetables are added to the mixture, they must be as dry as possible before being incorporated in the dough; fresh herbs need to be chopped or finely minced.

Fresh pasta cooks very quickly and should be tender, but have a discernible texture, known as *al dente*. It is best to cook fresh pasta as close to service time as possible; however, it can be held successfully for banquet and buffet services.

Purchasing and Handling Nonperishable Foods

While *nonperishable*, or *staple*, items have relatively long shelf lives, the quality of these dry goods is better when they are fresh. Foods classified as staples include:

- Grains, meals, and flours
- Dried legumes, pasta, noodles, herbs, and spices
- Nuts, seeds, and sweeteners
- Condiments, oils, and shortenings
- Coffee, tea, and baking supplies
- Cooking wines, liqueurs, and cordials

Professional kitchens maintain a *par stock* (the amount of stock necessary to cover operating needs between deliveries) of dry goods, and sometimes a slight overstock to cover emergencies. Precautions must be taken to avoid understocking and overstocking. Upon delivery, all bags, boxes, and containers must be inspected, then properly stored in clean, accessible, and well-ventilated storage areas. All goods should be placed above floor level, on shelving or pallets. Whole grains, nuts, seeds, and coffee (non-vacuum-packed) should be refrigerated.

Grains, meals, and flours are of primary importance in cooking. Whole grains have a shorter shelf life than milled grains and should be purchased in quantities that can be used within three weeks.

Oils are pressed from foods such as olives, nuts, corn, avocados, or soybeans. When oil has been *hydrogenated*, a process that causes it to remain solid at room temperature, it becomes shortening. Several different oils and shortenings are required in the professional kitchen. The chef must determine what shortening or oil is suitable for a particular dish or cooking method. Oils and shortenings should be stored in a dry place, away from extremes of heat and light.

Vinegars and condiments are essential both as ingredients and as accompaniments to food, and must be held in dry storage, away from heat and light.

Dried herbs and spices are used to enhance the flavor of food; however, they can easily lose their flavor and potency. Spices and herbs should be purchased in quantities that will be used within three months. Never store spices or herbs on top of the range or stove. Whole spices can keep their flavor for about six months if they are stored in a cool, dry spot, protected from direct heat and light. The same rules apply to salt and pepper. In very humid weather, a few grains of rice added to salt containers will prevent the salt from clumping. Whole peppercorns will retain their flavor indefinitely.

Wines, cordials, and liquors bought for cooking and baking should be of the same quality as those purchased for drinking. Preserve the flavor by keeping them refrigerated, in tightly closed bottles, or in bottles fitted with pouring spouts.

The amount of prepared, canned, and frozen foods kept on hand depends on the chef's judgment and the restaurant's requirements. All stock should be rotated according to the FIFO method.

Progress Check 4

Complete the following statements by writing the correct word or words in each blank. Check your answers against the answer key for Progress Check 4 on p. 59.

1. Potatoes to be pureed must first be ____________________ by boiling, steaming, or baking.

2. Whipped or mashed potatoes should be held for service in a ____________________.

3. Fresh pasta dough can be mixed in three ways: by hand, in a food processor, or in an ____________________.

4. Both dried and fresh pasta should be cooked only to the point of ____________________.

5. ____________________ is the best cooking method for retaining vegetables' vitamins and minerals.

6. Scalloped and au gratin are examples of potato dishes prepared ____________________.

7. In the ____________________ method, grains remain separate and have a nutty flavor.

8. ____________________ is the amount of stock necessary to cover operating needs between deliveries.

9. ____________________ works by causing a food's molecules to vibrate, creating a friction that heats the food.

10. For best results when making soufflé potatoes, use potatoes with a high ____________________ content and a low ____________________ content.

DAIRY PRODUCTS, HORS D'OEUVRES, AND SALADS

Purchasing and Preparing Dairy Products and Breakfast Foods

Most cuisines rely heavily on dairy products and eggs. With a high concentration of protein and calcium, dairy products and eggs are important as individual menu items as well as key ingredients in many preparations. These highly perishable foods must be purchased and stored carefully. One important point: *milk and cream from separate containers should never be combined*. The freshness periods are different and contamination could occur. Dairy products tend to absorb other flavors quickly and easily, so they should be stored separately and properly covered. Cheeses should be wrapped as airtight as possible to preserve moistness and avoid flavor transfer. When milk and cream are used in hot dishes, they should be at boiling temperature before the chef adds them to other ingredients.

The egg is the chef's magic ingredient and is one of the most versatile and essential foods. Eggs can be used for thickening, coloring, adding moisture, forming emulsions, foaming, and enriching other foods. An egg is composed of the outer shell, the white, and the yolk. The white consists of protein and water; the yolk contains protein, fat, and lecithin, a natural emulsifier. The USDA grade AA egg means that the egg is fresh, with a white that will not spread unduly when the shell is broken and a yolk that rides high on the white's surface.

Eggs are available in six sizes—jumbo, extra large, large, medium, small, and pee wee. Younger hens produce smaller eggs which are generally higher in quality than jumbo eggs. Medium eggs are best for breakfast entrées where appearance is important. Egg substitutes, necessary for cholesterol-free diet requirements, are either egg-free or made with egg whites.

Eggs should be inspected carefully upon delivery, and any shells that are cracked or dirty should be discarded because of the high contamination risk. In addition, eggs should be refrigerated and the stock rotated.

Milk is invaluable as a beverage and as a key ingredient. It is available in various forms and is classified according to its percentage of fat and milk solids. Cream is the fatty component of milk. There are two kinds of cream—heavy or whipping cream, and light cream. Some chefs prefer to use cream that has not been ultrapasteurized because they believe it will whip to a greater volume.

To be labeled *ice cream*, a product must contain a certain amount of milkfat. Vanilla ice cream must contain no less than 10 percent milkfat; other flavors must contain at least 8 percent. Quality ice cream has a custard base (cream and/or milk and eggs), melts readily in the mouth, and does not weep or separate when it softens at room temperature.

Butter is made by stirring cream that contains between 30 and 45 percent milkfat at a high speed. Sweet butter means that only sweet cream was used. Butter must be stored in tightly sealed containers to prevent flavor transfer.

The variety of cheeses ranges from milk to sharp to pungent. The type of milk used determines the cheese's flavor and texture. Following are a number of categories of cheese and an example of each:

- Fresh cheese (cottage cheese)
- Semi-soft cheese (Edam)
- Soft cheese (Brie)
- Grating cheese (Parmesan)
- Hard cheese (cheddar)
- Blue-veined cheese (Roquefort)

Breakfast Foods

Breakfast is fast becoming a very profitable and busy service for contemporary restaurants. Breakfast cookery involves competency in preparing egg dishes, breakfast meats, breads, hot and cold cereals, and beverages. Besides brunch, many of these items, including quiches and omelets, are carried over to lunch and dinner. Egg cookery includes several techniques—boiled, baked poached, fried, scrambled, omelets, and soufflés. (See Exhibit 9.) It is important to practice sanitation and safety procedures when handling, sorting, and cooking eggs.

Boiled eggs are actually simmered. Violent boiling can cause fragile eggshells to crack. In addition to their role in breakfast menus, boiled eggs are used in a number of other preparations—in cold hors d'oeuvres, canapés, salads, and garnishes.

For perfect hard-boiled eggs, follow these tips:

- Use enough water to completely submerge the eggs.
- Lower the eggs into the water prior to simmering, instead of dropping them.
- Reduce the heat under the pot once a simmer is reached.
- Cool and peel hard-cooked eggs immediately after they have finished cooking to prevent a green ring from forming around the yolk.

EXHIBIT 9—COOKING TIMES FOR EGGS PREPARED IN THE SHELL

COOKING STYLE	TIME	COMMENTS
Coddled	30 seconds	Lower cold eggs into already simmering water
Soft-boiled	1 to 2 minutes	
Medium-boiled	3 to 5 minutes	
Hard-boiled	10 minutes	Variation on technique calls for eggs to be removed from heat when water reaches a boil, covered, and allowed to remain in hot water for 20 to 30 minutes

Baked eggs include a number of preparations. The egg is baked with a variety of fillings in a container. Changing the size, shape, and material of the baking dish can affect the texture of the finished egg. Most important, the egg must be fresh to prevent the yolk from breaking.

Poached eggs are popular in classic dishes such as Eggs Benedict and Eggs Florentine, as toppings for hash or baked potatoes, and as single items. A properly poached egg should be tender and well shaped; the yolk should be centered; and the white should not be ragged.

Frying is a popular way to prepare eggs. To make sure that eggs are fried with the yolks high and centered, it is essential to use the correct heat level, perfectly fresh eggs, and an appropriate amount of cooking fat. The yolk should be cooked to the required doneness—slightly runny for "easy;" slightly thickened but still flowing for "medium;" completely set for "hard."

Scrambled eggs are fast and easy for the chef. Perfect scrambled eggs should have a light texture, creamy consistency, and delicate flavor—and they must be served very hot. To achieve this, the eggs should be blended just until the yolks and whites are combined, and then any seasonings should be added. Scrambled eggs must be cooked over gentle heat, stirred constantly, and scraped from the pan's bottom and sides to be creamy.

Omelets are either rolled, flat, or souffléed. A rolled omelet should be golden-yellow with a creamy, moist interior and must be made to order. Flat omelets may be made as individual portions or in larger quantities. Souffléed omelets have a light fluffy texture that is achieved by incorporating air into the eggs.

A popular egg dish that can be carried over to lunch or dinner is a *quiche*. A quiche is basically a custard baked in a crust. Eggs are blended with milk or cream until smooth; seasonings and garnish are added; the mixture is poured into a prepared crust, baked in a moderate oven, and served hot. Quiches can be reheated in a microwave oven just before service.

Soufflés are not strictly for breakfast. In reality, they are rarely served for breakfast because they take time to bake and can only be made to order. Savory and dessert soufflés are not difficult to prepare, but timing is everything. Soufflés must be served while they are piping hot and puffy.

Other popular breakfast foods include pancakes, crêpes, waffles, and French toast. The batters for these items are simple to make and many recipes can be prepared a day in advance. Each can be cooked in a few minutes.

Breakfast meats, such as bacon, sausage, ham, and breakfast steaks complete the meal. Bacon should be cooked until crisp and properly drained. Pre-cooked sausage and breakfast links cook quickly.

Hash is a mixture of chopped meats, potatoes, and onions. The ratio of meat to vegetable is not an exact one, and the chef can include a wide variety of vegetables to give the dish color and flavor.

Fish, such as smoked salmon or trout, is a popular breakfast and brunch item. Potatoes can be prepared in a variety of ways for breakfast and brunch. Fruits and breads (including muffins, quick breads, English muffins, and bagels) are a tradition at breakfast, served hot or cold.

Traditional breakfast beverages include coffee and tea, but juice, hot chocolate, and milk- or juice-based blender drinks are gaining notice. Brewed coffee does not hold well for more than 45 minutes to an hour, unless it is held in a vacuum container. Like coffee, tea should always be served hot and steaming.

Hors d'oeuvres and Appetizers

Many times it is the first course that forms a guest's impression of an entire operation and its service, yet sometimes the importance of these dishes is overlooked. There are no unimportant parts of a meal; hors d'oeuvres and appetizers must be of high quality and nutritiously prepared.

Hors d'oeuvres are foods that are served separately from the main meal—either before the meal or in place of the meal. Hors d'oeuvres should complement the main course and may be cold or hot, served as finger foods, or require the use of a plate and fork. They should be fresh, small enough to eat in a bite or two, and attractively served.

Hors d'oeuvres should be tailored to suit the needs and abilities of the kitchen and dining room staff and the nature of the event. Finger foods are perfect for outdoor receptions or any reception where guests will not be seated. The food should be self-contained—once it is consumed, there should be nothing for the guest to discard. Various types of hors d'oeuvres include crudités, canapés, and hot puff pastry or phyllo dough.

Crudités served with dips are among the most popular finger foods. Vegetables used must be well chilled and cut in appropriately small pieces. *Canapés* are small, open-faced sandwiches. Traditional canapés contain a bread base cut into assorted shapes, a filling, and a garnish. Contemporary canapés use other bases, such as crackers, firm vegetables (cucumbers, peppers), and pastry dough.

Cold hors d'oeuvres often include a sauce or are served with a sauce, and require serving utensils. They are best suited to buffet service or as part of a meal. One or two hot hors d'oeuvres are often included to give the impression of substance. Popular items include foods encased in a pastry dough that may be eaten without a fork, provided a sauce is not an accompaniment. The type of hors d'oeuvres, as well as the requirements of the function, determine how the foods will be presented—using elegant butler service, a casual buffet service, or a combination.

Appetizers are intended as the introduction to a meal, and the chef should remember the following points:

- Keep the portion size appropriate. The guest should still be able to enjoy the full meal.
- Use fresh herbs and seasonings judiciously. Don't overwhelm the palate for the dishes that are to follow.
- Pay special attention to presentation. Foods must be served at the proper temperature with a minimum of garnish.

Salads

The salad selection on the contemporary menu goes far beyond the simple dinner salad, and the salad has gone beyond a first course into a main entrée at lunch or dinner. Greens should be selected and prepared carefully—tender delicate lettuces can be overwhelmed by more robust greens. The green salad is one of the most abused items on the menu, and deserves the same attention to detail, preparation, and quality as any other dish. The chef should keep in mind the range of individual flavors, textures, and colors of lettuces and other greens to produce a well-balanced, attractive salad.

To properly prepare greens, the following points are essential:

- Hold greens under refrigeration until they are to be prepared and served.
- Clean all greens scrupulously to remove all traces of sand, grit, and insects.
- Dry the greens as thoroughly as possible after rinsing.
- Remove any tough stems or wilted spots. Tearing is preferred for delicate greens, but the leaves must not be bruised.
- Greens should not have to be cut by the patron. The preferred serving size for a piece of lettuce is about the size of half of a dollar bill.

- Dress greens appropriately, with only enough dressing to lightly coat them. The normal ratio is one-third ounce of dressing per ounce of greens.

The salad dressing's flavor should be appropriate to the salad ingredients. The basic dressings are vinaigrette, emulsified vinaigrette, and mayonnaise. *Vinaigrettes* are most suitable for contemporary menus. The recipe for basic vinaigrette includes approximately three parts oil to one part vinegar. The ingredients should be remixed just before serving. *Emulsified vinaigrette* dressings and light mayonnaise dressings are thick and coat the ingredients more heavily. They are especially effective and flavorful for salads that include ingredients such as grains, pastas, meat, or fish. Emulsified vinaigrette dressing has the same ratio of major ingredients as basic vinaigrette, with the addition of egg yolks.

Mayonnaise is the most stable of emulsified dressings. It contains a higher ratio of oil to vinegar and a greater quantity of egg yolks than is required for an emulsified vinaigrette. Perfect mayonnaise is creamy, pale ivory, but not too thick. Other dressings may be made by using the three main types as a base.

Progress Check 5

Complete the following statements by writing the correct word or words in each blank. Check your answers against the answer key for Progress Check 5 on p. 59.

1. Milk comes in various forms and is classified according to its percentage of ____________ and ____________.

2. An example of blue-veined cheese is ____________; an example of fresh cheese is ____________ cheese.

3. The three basic omelet styles are ____________, ____________, and ____________.

4. To be labeled ice cream, a product must contain a certain amount of ____________.

5. For optimum quality, salad dressings should not be held for longer than ____________ days.

6. A ____________ is basically a custard baked in a crust.

7. ____________ are bite-sized foods that are served separately from the meal—either before the meal or in place of a meal.

8. The first course of a main meal is traditionally called the ____________.

9. Three basic dressing categories for salads are ____________, ____________, and ____________.

10. The normal ratio of dressing to greens is ____________ of dressing per ____________ of greens.

BAKERY PRODUCTS

Managing the Quantity Bakery

Baking is a science in which exact measurements, combined with the proper handling of ingredients and equipment, are essential to ensure quality. Baking mise en place includes basic techniques that provide the foundation for the pastry chef.

Baking ingredients fall into six categories:

- Strengtheners, such as flour and eggs
- Shorteners, such as butters and oils
- Sweeteners, such as sugars and syrups
- Different flavorings, such as vanilla and nuts
- Chemical and organic leaveners, such as baking powder
- Thickeners, such as cornstarch, flour, and eggs

Strengtheners provide stability and ensure that the baked item does not collapse once it is removed from the oven. The binding properties of *gluten*, a protein found in flour, are responsible for a light, even texture in the finished product. *Sweeteners* add flavor and moisture. The caramelization of sugar is responsible for the attractive brown color that appears on many baked items.

Leaveners fall into three categories: chemical, organic, and physical. Baking soda and baking powder are the main chemical leaveners; yeasts comprise the organic leaveners; the basic physical leavener is steam. *Thickeners* include gelatin, flour, arrowroot, corn starch, and eggs. Thickeners, combined with the stirring process, determine the finished product's properties. For example, custard cooked over direct heat and stirred constantly will result in a sauce; the same custard recipe cooked in a bain-marie with no stirring will set into a firm custard that can be sliced.

Flavorings—such as vanilla, almond, nuts, and dried fruit—do not affect an item's texture.

One of the most important elements in baking is *scaling*, or the careful measuring of all ingredients. To be absolutely accurate, all items are measured by weight, including the finished dough. Once the batter or dough is mixed, it is scaled once more to ensure that the proper amount is used for the pan size.

Dry ingredients must be sifted before they are incorporated into the dough or batter. *Sifting* aerates flour and confectioners' sugar, removing lumps and filtering out any impurities. Sifting should be done once the ingredients have been properly scaled.

Baking pans must be properly selected and prepared. The correct shape and size are important to ensure that the baked item's texture and appearance are correct. Delicate batters must be baked in pans that are liberally greased (usually with a hydrogenated shortening or a blend of shortening and flour) and floured. Lean doughs very often are dusted with cornmeal, while angel food cakes are baked in completely grease-free tube pans.

It is also important that the proper oven is used. The oven must not be overloaded during baking, or the air will not be able to circulate and bake the items properly. Once the baked item has been removed from the oven, it must be cooled on a rack in the baking pan. The baked items can be served or appropriately stored.

Chocolate is a delicate ingredient that must be handled with care. Chocolate contains two distinct types of fat that melt at different temperatures. To ensure even, smooth handling, it is melted in a process called *tempering*. The chocolate is melted and removed from the heat at a certain temperature. Then more chocolate is added and placed on the heat again. Tempered chocolate will coat items with an even layer and then harden into a shiny shell.

Baking Yeast Products

Yeast breads are divided into two categories—*lean doughs* and *rich doughs*. Lean doughs are made with flour, yeast, and water; rich doughs are produced with the addition of shortening or tenderizing ingredients such as sugars, syrups, butter, eggs, milk, or cream. When these fats are introduced, they change the bread's overall texture, as well as the way the dough is handled. Breads made from lean dough tend to have a chewier texture, more bite, and a crisp crust. Rich doughs should have a cake-like texture after baking (for example, Parker House rolls and cloverleaf rolls).

Dry yeast and fresh yeast are organic leaveners that should be proofed if there is any doubt about whether the yeast is "alive." *Proofing* is done before the yeast is added to the other ingredients.

To proof yeast:

- Combine the yeast with warm liquid and a small amount of flour or sugar.
- Let the mixture rest at room temperature until a thick surface foam forms. The foam indicates that the yeast is alive and can be used. If there is no foam, the yeast is dead and should be discarded.

Sponge and sourdough starter are two types of yeast batter. *Sponge* is used with certain flours such as rye and oat that are low in gluten; *sourdough* is leavened with a fermented starter instead, or in addition to, fresh yeast.

The primary technique used for mixing yeast dough is the *straight dough method*, and is applicable to all types of doughs—lean, rich, and sponge.

Once the dough is in the pan, it must be allowed to rise a second time. This is called *bench proofing*. The dough should not be allowed to rise too much during bench proofing because it will continue to rise slightly when it bakes in the oven. This is called *oven spring*. The doneness of baked goods is determined by color and size. (See Exhibit 10.)

Following are some tips on preparing and baking yeast products:

- If the baked item tastes strongly of yeast, the dough was not allowed sufficient time to proof before baking, or too much yeast was used.
- Doughs that do not have sufficient salt will have a bland flavor.
- If the dough is pale after baking, it is either not completely baked or has been baked at too low a temperature.

EXHIBIT 10—COMMON PROBLEMS WITH YEAST BREADS AND THEIR PROBABLE CAUSES

FAULTS	Improper mixing	Insufficient salt	Too much salt	Dough weight too much for pan	Dough weight too light for pan	Insufficient yeast	Dough overproofed	Dough underproofed	Dough temperature too high	Dough temperature too low	Dough too stiff	Proof box too hot	Green flour	Dough chilled	Too much sugar	Insufficient sugar	Dough too young	Dough too old	Improper molding	Insufficient shortening	Oven temperature too high	Oven temperature too low	Over-baked
Lack of volume	√		√		√	√		√						√			√	√			√		
Too much volume		√		√			√											√				√	
Crust color too pale										√		√				√		√					
Crust color too dark										√					√		√				√		
Crust blisters													√				√	√	√				
Shelling of top crust								√			√		√			√							
Poor keeping qualities		√					√		√		√					√		√		√		√	
Poor texture, crumbly							√					√					√	√				√	
Crust too thick																√		√				√	√
Streaky crumb																			√				
Gray crumb								√	√			√											
Lack of shred							√										√	√					
Coarse grain	√				√		√			√							√	√	√				
Poor taste and flavor		√							√									√					

Reprinted with permission from *The Baker's Manual*, 4th ed., by Joseph P. Amendola. New York: Van Nostrand Reinhold, 1993.

Quick Breads, Cakes, and Pastries

Quick breads, such as muffins, biscuits, scones, and soda breads, differ from yeast breads in that they use chemical leaveners rather than organic ones and do not require a rising period. There are four basic methods for preparing batters:

- The *straight mix method*—All ingredients are combined at once and blended into a batter.
- The *creaming method*—Fat and sugar are creamed together for an exceptionally fine crumb and dense, rich texture.
- The *two-stage method*—This method is used to prepare high-ratio cakes. First, the dry ingredients are combined with all of the shortening and half of the liquid until smooth, then the remaining wet ingredients are gradually added.
- The *foaming method*—A foam of whole eggs or their yolks or whites provides the structure for cakes with the lightest texture, such as angel food and chiffon cakes.

Steamed puddings and dessert soufflés are batters that require different handling. Steamed puddings are more stable because of the greater percentage of eggs and sugar in the batter. Soufflés rely much more on egg whites and are not as stable.

Basic pie dough is sometimes called 3-2-1 dough because it is composed of three parts flour, two parts fat, and one part water (by weight). It is important to use pastry flour and to work the dough as little as possible. Fat and liquid should both be cold. The fat used is shortening, butter, or lard; the liquid is usually water, but sometimes milk or cream is substituted. If these ingredients are used instead of water, the amount of fat in the overall formula should be decreased.

In general, pies are baked just until they begin to take on a golden color.

Here are some tips on preparing and baking quick breads, cakes, and pastries:

- If the dough has been rolled out unevenly, the thicker portions may appear moist, indicating that the dough is not fully baked.
- The dough should be flaky. If the dough has been underbaked, the texture may be gummy or rubbery. If it has been overbaked, the crust may be tough.
- Pie dough made with vegetable shortening will have a neutral flavor. Butter or a butter/shortening combination will introduce the butter flavor.

Pies are usually double-crusted, while tarts usually have a single crust. Fruit fillings are generally used for pies, tarts, and strudels. They are prepared using sliced and peeled fresh fruit. The fruit is either poached with a liquid or allowed to cook as the entire pastry bakes. Cornstarch or arrowroot may be added to thicken the fruit filling.

Roll-in doughs are used for Danish, croissant, and puff pastry. Proper mixing methods, rolling techniques, and temperature control are necessary to produce a flaky, quality product. The dough must be rolled out into a large rectangle, with butter rolled out to the correct dimensions. The dough is then folded over the roll-in, rolled again, and folded the appropriate number of times. A few guidelines when working with this dough:

- Keep the dough chilled.
- Use a sharp knife when shaping or cutting the edge.
- Do not run the roller over the dough's edge.
- Chill puff-pastry items before baking them.
- Save puff-pastry scraps for use in other smaller items.

Other doughs, such as phyllo and pâté à choux are commonly used. *Phyllo dough* is used to prepare strudel and baklava and is a very lean dough. *Pâté à choux* is made by combining water, butter, flour, and eggs into a smooth butter. Some familiar desserts that use this method include éclairs and cream puffs.

Cookies should be bite-size and, because of their high sugar content, are best when baked in convection ovens.

Creams and Desserts

Sauces are used to add flavor, moisture, and eye appeal to desserts. Vanilla sauce, also known as *crême anglaise,* is a classic accompaniment to soufflés and steamed puddings. It is a delicate sauce that must be handled carefully. It is especially important to have all the necessary equipment assembled before beginning. If the sauce should begin to overheat or curdle, it can still be saved by straining it immediately into a container set in an ice-water bath.

Other popular sauces include caramel, butterscotch, chocolate, and fruit sauces. Any of these sauces can be prepared in advance.

Pastry creams are denser than custards and are frequently used as the filling for eclairs. It may also be used as a soufflé base. Eggs, sugar, flour, milk, and/or cream are cooked together into a very thick, smooth mixture. Pastry cream, as a basic preparation, is part of the mise en place for many kitchen desserts.

Delicate *Bavarian creams* are made by stabilizing a vanilla sauce with gelatin, combined with whipped cream and beaten egg whites. They may be used as single items, or as fillings for a variety of pastries.

Other popular desserts are frozen soufflés, mousses, ice creams, sorbets, sherbets, and granites. Poached fruits include such favorites as peach Melba and Belle Helene. Usually fruits to be poached must be firm enough to hold their shape during cooking. Very tender fruits such as berries or bananas are not suited for this technique. The greater the amount of sugar in the poaching liquid, the more firm the end result will be. The use of wine as part or all of the poaching liquid will have a similar effect. Sauces, creams, and fruits are most often used as icings, fillings, or decorations for special pastries, such as elegant tortes or layer cakes.

Progress Check 6

Complete the following statements by writing the correct word or words in each blank. Check your answers against the answer key for Progress Check 6 on p. 59.

1. ____________________ ensure that a baked item does not collapse once it is removed from the oven.

2. Flattening yeast dough after proofing to expel carbon dioxide gas and stabilize the temperature is known as ____________________.

3. Allowing yeast dough to rise a second time is called ____________________.

4. The ____________________ calls for all ingredients to be combined at once and blended into a batter.

5. The ____________________ is used to prepare products with more refined crumb and texture.

6. Basic pie dough is often called 3-2-1 dough because it is composed of three parts ____________________, two parts ____________________, and one part ____________________.

7. ____________________ is the dough most commonly used to create cream puffs and éclairs.

8. ____________________ is used to prepare strudel and baklava, and is a very ____________________ dough.

9. ____________________ are used in the creation of napoleons, éclairs, and Boston cream pie.

10. A delicate cream made with vanilla sauce, gelatin, whipped cream, and beaten egg whites is called ____________________ cream.

TEST YOUR KNOWLEDGE

Mark the best answer to each of the following questions by circling the appropriate letter.

1. The best temperatures in which to store meat and poultry are:

   a. 25°F–32°F (-4°C–0°C)
   b. 32°F–36°F (0°C–2°C)
   c. 36°F–40°F (2°C–4°C)
   d. 40°F–45°F (4°C–7°C)

2. The best temperatures in which to store fresh eggs are:

   a. 25°F–32°F (-4°C–0°C)
   b. 32°F–36°F (0°C–2°C)
   c. 36°F–40°F (2°C–4°C)
   d. 40°F–45°F (4°C–7°C)

3. The proper way to store fresh produce is to:

   a. place it in a well-lit, ventilated room.
   b. peel, wash, trim, and refrigerate it.
   c. leave it whole until needed.
   d. keep all produce together in the refrigerator.

4. In which cooking method is the food first seared in hot oil and then slowly cooked in liquid?

   a. Sautéing.
   b. Stewing.
   c. Swim-frying.
   d. Braising.

5. *Forcemeat* is an emulsion of:

   a. lean meat and bread crumbs.
   b. lean meat and fat.
   c. fatty meat and egg whites.
   d. fatty meat and vegetables.

6. The *most* reliable method of determining doneness in roasted foods is to:

   a. check the color of the food.
   b. insert a kitchen fork.
   c. use an instant-reading thermometer.
   d. cut a small slice of meat and taste it.

7. Fish should be gutted immediately because:

   a. there could be toxins in the viscera.
   b. it is easier to scale and trim for pan dressing.
   c. enzymes will break down the flesh, leading to spoilage.
   d. the viscera will develop an unpleasant odor.

8. Shoulder cuts of meat are best suited for which cooking technique?

   a. Braising.
   b. Grilling.
   c. Sautéing.
   d. Roasting.

9. The purpose of trussing a bird is to:

   a. give it a shape that will cook evenly.
   b. ensure the stuffing remains in the bird.
   c. make a large bird look smaller.
   d. fit several birds in one roasting pan.

10. The best way to decide on the most appropriate cooking method for fish is to consider the:

    a. sauce.
    b. shortening used.
    c. flavor.
    d. flesh.

11. Which of the following is an example of a grand sauce?

    a. Demi-glacé.
    b. Jus lié.
    c. Jus.
    d. Beurre blanc.

12. Which of the following is the best way to clarify beef broth that has become cloudy?

    a. Add vinegar.
    b. Add more liquid.
    c. Boil a second time.
    d. Add egg whites.

13. Lower-grade fruits should:

    a. be used in baked pies and puddings.
    b. never be purchased by foodservice operations.
    c. be used as garnishes.
    d. be substituted for frozen fruits.

14. Nonperishable items should be stored:

    a. under refrigeration.
    b. on the floor, in a dry corner.
    c. without ventilation.
    d. above floor level, on shelves.

15. Which of the following fruits is most appropriate for poaching?

    a. Raspberries.
    b. Bananas.
    c. Strawberries.
    d. Pears.

16. Pasta should be cooked until it is:

    a. al dente.
    b. au jus.
    c. golden in color.
    d. a l'anglaise.

17. Of the following, the best way to cook vegetables for to-order service is:

    a. deep-frying.
    b. stir-frying.
    c. steaming.
    d. baking.

18. In general, the best color is retained when vegetables are:

    a. cooked in a butter sauce.
    b. cooked quickly over high heat.
    c. simmered gently in water.
    d. cooked for as short a time as possible.

19. It is best to start boiling potatoes in:

    a. simmering liquid.
    b. boiling liquid.
    c. lukewarm liquid.
    d. cold liquid.

20. To prevent peeled potatoes from discoloration, they should be:

    a. sprinkled with salt.
    b. lightly covered in a neutral oil.
    c. held submerged in a liquid.
    d. simmered for two minutes.

21. Dried herbs should be stored:

    a. on the stove top.
    b. away from heat.
    c. under refrigeration.
    d. indefinitely.

22. Which of the following is the fastest way to reheat vegetables without losing color or nutrients?

    a. Stir-frying.
    b. Sautéing.
    c. Deep-frying.
    d. Microwaving.

23. Which of the following vegetables can be sautéed or stir-fried from their raw state?

    a. Green beans.
    b. Summer squash.
    c. Carrots.
    d. Cauliflower.

24. Most vegetables lose their quality in storage after:

    a. three or four hours.
    b. one day.
    c. three or four days.
    d. one week.

25. Milk, cream, and butter should be stored separately from other goods because they:
    a. are more perishable than other foods.
    b. absorb other flavors easily.
    c. must be kept at warmer temperatures.
    d. are used according to the FIFO principle.

26. Whole, shelled eggs can be safely stored for how long?
    a. 2 to 3 days.
    b. 5 to 7 days.
    c. 2 to 3 weeks.
    d. 1 to 2 months.

27. When yeast bread has a crust that is too pale, it is most likely caused by using:
    a. the wrong type of flour.
    b. too much sugar.
    c. too low a cooking temperature.
    d. too many eggs.

28. When a pie crust is too tough, it is most likely caused by:
    a. overmixing.
    b. too much shortening.
    c. a baking temperature that is too low.
    d. a baking temperature that is too high.

29. Quick breads differ from yeast breads in that they:
    a. use chemical leaveners.
    b. use organic leaveners.
    c. must be punched down three times.
    d. are baked in a bain-marie.

30. An example of a *physical* leavener is:
    a. baking powder.
    b. yeast.
    c. baking soda.
    d. steam.

ANSWER KEYS

Progress Checks

Progress Check 1 Answers

1. cross-contamination
2. utility
3. protein
4. sanitizing
5. 45, 140
6. carbohydrates
7. dry-heat
8. moist-heat cooking
9. indirect heat
10. moist, plump

Progress Check 2 Answers

1. forequarter, hindquarter
2. loin
3. offal
4. fabrication
5. yield grade
6. au jus
7. en papillote
8. shellfish
9. well-done
10. round, flat, nonbony

Progress Check 3 Answers

1. Hollandaise
2. demi-glacé, velouté, béchamel, tomato, Hollandaise
3. clear
4. emulsion
5. reduction
6. roux
7. fumet
8. jus lié
9. glacé, glaze
10. clear, thick

Progress Check 4 Answers

1. parcooked
2. bain-marie
3. electric mixer
4. al dente
5. steaming
6. en casserole
7. risotto
8. par stock
9. microwaving
10. starch, moisture

Progress Check 5 Answers

1. fat, milk solids
2. Roquefort, cottage
3. rolled, flat, soufléed
4. milkfat
5. three
6. quiche
7. hors d' oeuvres
8. appetizer
9. vinaigrette, emulsified vinaigrette, mayonnaise
10. one-third ounce, ounce

Progress Check 6 Answers

1. strengtheners
2. punching down
3. bench proofing
4. straight-mix method
5. creaming method
6. flour, fat, water
7. pâté à choux
8. phyllo dough, lean
9. pastry creams
10. Bavarian

Test Your Knowledge

1. b
2. c
3. c
4. d
5. b
6. c
7. c
8. a
9. a
10. d
11. a
12. d
13. a
14. d
15. d
16. a
17. c
18. d
19. d
20. c
21. b
22. d
23. b
24. c
25. b
26. b
27. c
28. d
29. a
30. d

GLOSSARY

Bouquet garni	Small bundle of herbs used to flavor stocks and soups
Butterfly	To cut an item, usually meat or seafood, and open out the edges to look like a butterfly
Dumpling	Any of a number of small, soft-dough or batter items that are steamed, poached, or simmered
Emulsion	Mixture of two or more liquids, one a fat or oil and the other water-based, so that one is suspended in the other
En papillote	Variation of steaming in which the items are encased in parchment paper and cooked in a hot oven
Fabrication	Working with the primal cuts of meat, fish, or poultry to make portion sizes or specialty cuts
Fermentation	Breakdown of carbohydrates into carbon dioxide gas and alcohol, usually through the action of yeast on sugar
Fillet	Boneless, skinless pieces of fish
Flat fish	Fish with a backbone running through its center with four fillets, two upper and two lower
Foodborne illness	Illness in humans caused by the consumption of an unwholesome or contaminated food product
Gluten	Protein found in flour that develops into long, elastic strands during the mixing and kneading process
Grain	Fruit of a grass
Kneading	Method of working and handling yeast dough
Legume	Seeds of certain plants, including beans and peas
Market form	Cuts of meat ready for sale
Meringue	Mixture of egg whites and sugar beaten until thickened
Mirepoix	Combination of chopped aromatic vegetables—usually two parts onion, one part carrot, and one part celery—used to flavor stocks, soups, and stews
Mise en place	Preparation and assembly of ingredients, pans, utensils, and plates or serving pieces needed for a particular dish or service period
Mollusk	Any of a number of invertebrate animals with soft, unsegmented bodies usually enclosed in a hard shell; includes clams, oysters, and snails

Parboil	Partially cook vegetables to be used in other preparations such as braises, grills, or gratins
Pastry bag	Plastic or paper decorating bag used to hold fondant or frosting to decorate cakes and pastry
Pathogen	Disease-causing micro-organism responsible for up to 95 percent of all foodborne illnesses
Pilaf	Grain dish in which the grain is first heated in a pan and then combined with hot liquid
Poêlé	Cook meat in its own juice in a covered vessel on a bed of vegetables; sometimes called *butter roasting*
Potentially hazardous foods	Foods capable of supporting disease-producing organisms and usually containing a high amount of protein
Primal cuts	First large meat cuts in butchering
Proofing	Second and/or third rising of fermentation stages in the making of yeast breads; also the initial rising of yeast in warm liquid to create a sponge
Round fish	Fish with a backbone along the upper edge with two fillets on either side
Sachet d' épices	Aromatic ingredients, encased in cheesecloth, used to flavor stocks and other liquids
Scaling	Measuring ingredients by weighing; dividing dough or batter into portions by weight
Sponge	Mixture prepared by combining yeast and liquid with a portion of flour and allowing it to ferment until it is light and spongy
Stock	Flavorful liquid made by gently simmering bones or vegetables in a liquid to extract their flavor, aroma, color, body, and nutritive value
Suprême	Boneless, skinless poultry breast
Temperature Danger Zone	Temperature range in which foods are most susceptible to contamination; 45°F to 140°F (7°C to 60°C)
Tempered chocolate	Chocolate that has been cooked so it will melt smoothly and harden evenly with a good shine
Trussing	Method of tying poultry to retain its shape for even cooking
Yeast	Microscopic fungus responsible for fermentation; an organic leavener necessary for making bread